Harmony and Balance in Living

Shawn Paul

Library of Congress Control Number (LCCN): 9781966647737

ISBNs:

eBook: 978-1-966647-71-3

Paperback: 978-1-966647-72-0

Hardback: 978-1-966647-73-7

Published by:

Authors Publishing House

178 Broadway, 3rd Floor, #1343

New York, NY 10001, USA

Main Line: (855) 624-0155

Email: support@authorspublishinghouse.com

Dedicated to all the compassionate, caring health professionals.

Table of Contents

Preface

A harmonious and balanced life exists when there is an integrated focus on all essential aspects of life. In the contemporary materialistic society, there is too much focus on hedonic pursuits and relatively less focus on spiritual pursuits. In Vedic culture, it is mentioned that we choose *preya* (pleasure) rather than *shreya* (joy, bliss). We seek *bhog* (enjoyment), not *yog* (bliss). We seek material progress instead of spiritual progress. The right balance is essential. The same concept in Buddhism emphasizes the middle way, which is between the two extremes of hedonistic pleasure and asceticism. Buddhism teaches that freedom and happiness will not be found in the extremes of either sensual indulgence or spiritual purification; a middle way is essential. It is the noble path that transcends these two extremes and leads to enlightenment, wisdom, and peace of mind. Western psychiatrist Sigmund Freud postulated three aspects of personality known as the id, the ego, and the superego. The Id is based on the pleasure principle, impulses, and instinct, while on the other end is the superego, stressing strict moral principles. Ego is negotiating balance between Id and super ego and is based on reality principles.

There needs to be a balance between freedom and responsibility; otherwise, there will be chaos in society. Balance is necessary between work and home life. Life will be full of peace, love, and joy if there is harmony and balance between physical, mental, emotional, and spiritual aspects of life.

In the U.S. society, there is plenty of food; two-thirds of the people are overweight, and one-third are obese. It takes a toll on physical health. Indulgence in too much eating, drinking, smoking, and the use of drugs is contributing to serious health problems. Teenagers spend too much time on Facebook, Nintendo games, and sexual pursuits at an early age, resulting in a lack of moral discipline to become responsible individuals. Basic life skills like interpersonal relationships and managing emotions appropriately are not addressed in the school setting. Parents are too busy making money, not realizing that quality time with children is essential to instill good values. There is a story in the news that a child saw his father boasting on TV that he charges $500.00 an hour for his time as a computer consultant. When his father came home, his child expressed his desire to borrow $250 from his father. Father readily gave him the money. The child had saved 250 earlier. He added $250 to $250 his father gave him and gave his father$ 500, requesting an hour of his time as his father's time was worth $500 an hour. The child's father came to his senses that moment and promised to spend quality time with his son.

There is a similar story narrated by an Indian sage to the audience during her spiritual discourse. She was called into a wealthy Indian family, where both physician parents worked hard. They had placed their son in the best nursery and provided his education in an elite university. After completing his law degree, the son informed his parents that he was leaving New York and moving to California, and this was the last time he saw them. The sage inquired from the young man his reason for deserting his family, who had sent him to the best nursery and elite university. His son told the sage that when his parents get old, he will send them to the best nursing home, lamenting that his parents were too busy making money and had spent little quality time with him during his growing-up years.

Many professional women at times feel guilty for not being able to have a balance between professional life and home life. One female lawyer was so busy building her career in the big law firm that she missed her child taking his first step to walk and other milestones in his development. She resigned from her job at a prestigious law firm and started working part-time from home. She felt satisfaction in balancing her family life with work.

There are many such instances when parents are too occupied making money, seeking fame and fortune, and have little or no time to guide their children in the right direction. There needs to be a balance between acquiring material wealth and spending quality time with the family.

Wellness is a state of harmony and balance between body, mind, and spirit. There needs to be a balance between nature and humans in society. There needs to be a balance between rich and poor through social justice; harmony between males and females, harmony between different religions, harmony between different nations, and harmony between different races and cultures.

Nature has a way of balancing itself. Day is followed by night. Homeostasis is a tendency toward a relatively stable equilibrium between independent elements. This is a process by which living things use to actually maintain a fairly stable condition necessary for survival. We need to have harmony within ourselves between our physical, mental, emotional, and spiritual aspects.

Evenness of mind is necessary to function properly. This book is intended to promote optimum health through having a harmonious and balanced life.

This book is divided into six sections. The first introductory section outlines the need to have harmony and balance within essential aspects of life. The second section emphasizes essential areas of physical health, consisting of a balanced diet, exercise, and adequate sleep. In this section, detailed information on steps for controlling blood pressure and lowering blood sugar is given. I have also included in this section information on complications from high cholesterol and changes you can make to lower your LDL cholesterol. Also included in this section are prevention measures for the top ten diseases in the U.S., including tips for weight control. I have incorporated ten exercises for every inch of your body in the exercise segment. Treatment for insomnia and behavior for a longer life summarizes the physical section.

The third section describes mental/ emotional health. Basic information on this subject is provided with specific guidelines for stress, anger, and anxiety management. Included are steps to deal with anger effectively. Relaxation techniques are described to improve mental/emotional well-being. List of essential social skills, work-life balance is incorporated for harmonious relationships. Included are steps to build healthy self-esteem and cultivate happiness. Rational Emotive Behavior Therapy (REBT) is illustrated for application in dealing with struggles in life, and this section concludes with six criteria for psychological well-being.

The fourth section comprises the spiritual health. Spiritual health and wellness are significant aspects of overall healthy well-being, as they envision an inner path enabling a person to discover the essence of their being. In this section, essential ways to find meaning and purpose in life are described.

The fifth section focuses on having global harmony and balance. This section transitions from individual wellness to global wellness. In this section, global disparity in health care is emphasized, and steps to improve health in developing countries are delineated.

The last section summary and conclusion integrate and culminate all essential aspects of harmonious and balanced living. This book ends with a holistic approach to having harmony and balance in living. It is the hope of this author that the book will enlighten the minds of its readers and subsequently help lead a peaceful and blissful life.

Section 1:
Introduction

Wellness is a state of being in good health- three intertwined components of body, mind, and spirit. The physical body is the foundation of healthy well-being. "Mens sana in corpore sano" is a classical Latin phrase that means "A healthy mind in a healthy body ". Further, if our limbic system (emotional mind) is aligned with the conscious mind (mental health), then there is a harmony between emotions and conscious thinking. When the mind is aligned with the spiritual realm, then blissfulness is achieved. Thus, harmony and balance between a healthy body, mind, and spirit will result in our holistic well-being. Righteous living is living consciously every moment with intentions and awareness. Shawn Paul, in his books "Religion without Boundaries" and "Religions, Spirituality and Humanity," delineated ten guiding principles focusing on physical, mental, emotional, and spiritual life through living consciously, meaningfully, and purposefully. Having a balanced life by respecting elders, loving our spouse, and taking good care of our children, providing them with good education, and instilling good values. Becoming compassionate and caring about others. Be conscious of our environment and become a proactive citizen. Taking responsibility is painful. Soul searching for self is also painful. It pains emotionally, but going through the process of pain comes real gain, realizing that we are responsible for our thoughts, feelings, and actions individually and collectively. We need to have a balance between freedom and responsibility. There needs to be a balance between nature, community, and human spirit. We need to be mindful of our responsibility to ourselves, our family, community, and nation, and be compassionate and caring to our brethren throughout the world.

Vedic Culture mentions four goals of a balanced life. They are known as *Purusharthas* (objectives of human lives). These four objectives are: *Dharma*(ethics), *Artha* (livelihood, wealth), *Kama* (sensual pleasure), and *Moksha* (liberation, freedom from the birth and rebirth cycle). If we can lead an honest living, balancing our moral duties and rights, enabling social order and right conduct with aesthetic enjoyment of life, affection, or love, then we will have a state of bliss and self-realization.

Abraham Maslow delineated five human needs that must be met for people to feel fulfilled in their lives. Maslow conceptualized both our physiological and psychological motives as different levels of priority. The different classes form a hierarchy of needs, in which lower-level needs have the first priority. Maslow presented these needs in the shape of a pyramid. The lowest level of Maslow's hierarchy, the base of the pyramid, is our physiological needs of food, shelter, and comfort. The next level of concern is satisfying safety and security needs. At the next level is love and belongingness. People need to feel connected to the social world and need to feel that they are loved and cherished for who they are as individuals. At the next level are self-esteem needs. People need to feel a sense of competence and achievement, that they are respected and valued by other people in their lives. At the fifth level is the need for self-actualization. People have a need to develop their unique potential. Maslow believed that the first four needs must be met in a relatively sequential fashion before moving on to higher needs. It is estimated that most of us are satisfied when our basic needs are met. Later in life, Maslow describes the sixth level as being intrinsic values such as truth, goodness, perfection, excellence, fairness, justice, etc. Sixth level transcend self-interest, considering wider holistic matters for the greater good. The same concept is in the Mahayana concept of bodhisattvas. Mahayana adherents take *bodhisattva* vows, working toward the liberation of all beings, rather than focusing only on personal liberation. This author prefers the *Mahayana* concepts and is a strong advocate of compassion and loving kindness toward others. In her book It Takes a Village, Hillary Clinton presents her vision for the children of America. She focused on the impact individuals and groups outside the family have, for better or worse, on a child's well-being, and advocates for a society that meets the needs of all children. This author extends that concept to a global level, where all rich countries and international organizations work together to uplift the lives of impoverished children throughout the globe. We need to have a balance between our lives and the lives of others who are less fortunate and lack basic needs.

Balance is essential in all aspects of our lives. The three interdependent aspects of life-physical, mental/emotional, and spiritual need to be in harmony and balance for a fulfilling life. The physical dimension has to do with the body, its functions, and the activities that support it. The mental dimension has to do with internal behavior. The dimension includes thoughts and attitudes. Thoughts originate in the mind. Attitudes are clusters of thoughts related to a subject theme. Mental health also includes intelligence and covers a broad range of topics, such as learning new skills, sharing abilities and ideas with others. It also includes occupation and how it complements your personality, values and abilities. The emotional realm relates to feelings. This realm is the vital part of everyone's life. Finally, the spiritual dimension is equally important as it refers to what individuals hold sacred in their lives. This component refers to innermost beliefs and sacred values the individual considers significant in his or her meaning and purpose of life. Spiritual aspects also include leading a noble life of honesty, empathy, compassion, and loving kindness. It is essential that these significant aspects of life be integrated with each other to have a harmonious and balanced life. After taking care of ourselves, we move on to take care of our family, community, nation, and global well-being. All of us, individually and collectively, can work together cohesively and compassionately to make positive impacts in our lives and the lives of others on the planet. This is the hope of this author that the information presented in this book will be valuable toward building a purposeful and meaningful life.

Section 2:
Physical Health

The human body is made up of thousands of complex chemical compounds. 70% of the body is composed of water. At the atomic level, six elements form 98% of the body mass: 61% oxygen, 23% carbon, 10% hydrogen, 2.64 % nitrogen, and 1.4% calcium and phosphorus. The remaining 2% of the mass consists of 44 other elements. After water, the most abundant substances in the body are our proteins, which make up approximately 20% of the human body. Then come organic salts, lipids, carbohydrates (sugar), and nucleic acids. Of these, there are DNA, known as the master planner for building the body, and RNA, which enables the body to follow these plans.

The body as a whole has been described as a combination of about 75 to 100 trillion cells, which play a specific role. A single cell does not function in isolation but in groups that form tissue. An organ is a collection of tissues that perform a specific function. The human body is the interplay of ten major systems as defined below:

1. The nervous system (NS) includes the brain, spinal cord, and nerves. The medical professional in this field is known as a neurologist.

2. The endocrine system is a coordination of body functions, ranging from the development of sexual characteristics to the release of hormones. The medical professional in this field is known as an endocrinologist

3. The Circulatory system consists of the heart, veins, arteries, and the blood that flows from them. The medical professional in this field is known as the cardiologist.

4. The Respiratory system includes the nose and throat, and the respiratory specialist known as a pulmonologist, and the ear, nose, and throat doctor known as an ENT Specialist.

5. The digestive system includes the mouth, teeth, stomach, intestines, liver, etc. The medical doctor in this field is known as the gastroenterologist.

6. The Muscle system is paired with the skeletal system.

7. The Skeletal system supports the body and contributes to the blood supply through bone marrow. The specialist in the muscles and skeletal system is known as an orthopedic doctor.

8. The reproductive system is the functioning of the organs pertaining to birth. The specialist in this field is known as an obstetrician and gynecologist (OB/GYN) physician.

9. The urinary system is ultimately linked with the condition that affects the urinary tract in men and women, and the diseases that affect the reproductive system. The specialist in this field is known as the urologist.

10. The skin system covers the outside of the body, including hair and nails. The medical specialist in this field is known as a dermatologist.

The physical body is the foundation of healthy well-being. The three pillars of good physical health- The balanced diet, regular exercise, and sufficient sleep work together to keep your body healthy.

Balanced Diet

We eat because we enjoy the taste and experience of different foods. Sharing food and meals are important social events. But other than pleasure, we need food to get nutrients and vitamins. Minerals and energy. There are seven essential components for a balanced diet: carbs, proteins, fat, fiber, vitamins, minerals, and water. Carbs, protein, and fat are three macronutrients in your diet.

% of daily calories & consumption	Function	Source
45-55%		
Carbs-For 2000 calories, between 900-1500 should be from carbohydrates. , equal to 225 to 325 g. of carbs a day	acts as an energy source. controls blood sugar involved in metabolism	wheat, maize, corn millet, oats, flour potatoes, fruit
Protein- 10-35%; for 2000 calories. 55g for men and 45 g for women. Higher for older people	Tissue growth and maintenance	meat, fish, and nuts eggs, pulse
Fat- 20-35%; 78-89 g fat per day	Energy, Hormones production	nuts, seeds, plant oil, dairy products

Essential information on Carbs, Protein, and Fat

Carbs: Simple and Complex

Carbohydrates are a large group of organic compounds that include sugar, starch, and cellulose, which can be broken down to release energy. Carbohydrates (carbs) form the basis of most diets, accounting for half of total energy intake. This food group can be separated into complex (good) and simple (bad) carbs. Complex carbs provide energy and are a key source of fiber, B vitamins, and minerals. Refined carbs (white flour, pasta, and rice) are digested more quickly by the body. This makes them a faster source of energy. Simple carbs are sugar. There can be natural (e.g., fructose forms in fruit) or refined (e.g., sucrose or glucose in soft drinks, cereal, and biscuits). Dr. David Kessler, MD, in his book Fast Carbs, Slow Carbs, concludes that processed food has become the cause of the global health crisis. In his book, he explained that the U.S. population is increasingly suffering from obesity and chronic diseases due to processed carbohydrates. Three major recommendations made by Dr. Kessler for dietary guidelines are:

1. Reduce consumption of fast carbs to gain control of weight and reduce the risk of metabolic disease.
2. Reduce blood lipids (especially LDL) by moving to a largely plant-based diet to markedly diminish the risk of cardiovascular disease.
3. Engage in daily moderate intensity exercise to control weight, increase metabolic flexibility, and reduce risk of metabolic and cardiovascular disease.

Fast carbs are rapidly absorbed and easy to overeat because they don't trigger feelings of fullness or satiety. They are primary ingredients in commercially available breakfast cereal, most types of bread, rolls, and pizza crust; anything made with processed flour, puffed or processed snacks, including a variety of chips and crackers. Slow carbs, by contrast, include legumes and non-starchy vegetables, such as leafy greens, cruciferous vegetables like broccoli and cauliflower, asparagus, bell Peppers, and tomatoes. These carbs are high in fiber and contain only a small amount of starch. Legumes, like beans, lentils, and chickpeas, contain naturally resistant starches because the fiber around the starch renders them most resistant to digestion. Though fruit contains sugars, mainly from fructose, fruit also contains fiber and micronutrients and is associated with improved control of blood glucose, blood pressure, and blood lipid, which lowers the risk of diabetes and cardiovascular disease.

One of the carb-related terms is the glycemic index (GI). This refers to how quickly the sugar is released into the bloodstream. Low (GI) foods release sugar slowly. This gives a prolonged supply of energy to the body. High GI food gives short bursts of energy.

Protein- Dietary protein is needed to supply amino acids for the growth and maintenance of our cells and tissues. The average adult requirement for protein is 0.83 grams of protein per kilogram of body weight per day. That would be 58 grams of protein per day for a 154-pound adult. Proteins are made up of many different amino acids linked together. Amino acids are classified as either essential or non-essential. Essential amino acids cannot be produced by the body and therefore come from the diet. Protein can be found in both plant-based and animal-based foods. In general, animal-based protein is of the highest quality as it contains higher proportions of essential amino acids compared to plant-based protein. For people who consume little or no animal-based food, such as vegans or vegetarians, it is important that they consume protein from sources such as rice, beans, chickpeas, and dairy products like milk and cheese.

FATS - Dietary fat is important for making healthy cells. It produces hormones and is a source of energy. Dietary intake for 2000 calories a day diet should not be more than 65 grams of fat, and out of that, less than 20 grams of saturated fat. Saturated fats are generally solid at room temperature, and these are the fats that will have a negative impact on health. They are found in butter, hard cheese, fatty meats and meat products, egg yolks, dairy products like whole milk, cream, lard, coconut, and palm oil. Saturated fat raises blood cholesterol more than anything else in the diet.

Unsaturated fats -This includes the Polyunsaturated, monounsaturated, and omega-3 fats. This will have a positive impact on our health. Monounsaturated fat is found in greater amounts in foods from plants, including olive oil and canola oil. Monounsaturated fat helps to reduce blood cholesterol. Polyunsaturated fat is a highly unsaturated fat that is found in food products derived from plants, including safflowers, sunflowers, and soybean oils. Like monounsaturated fat, it is a healthy alternative to saturated fat.

Trans fat is a form of unsaturated fat that rarely exists in natural food but is associated with partly hydrogenated vegetable oils. They are usually added to processed foods such as cakes and biscuits, and so they should be eaten less often in small amounts. Trans fat as cooking oil has been found in some regions. Trans fat is harmful to health.

Good fats, bad fats, and heart disease

Certain types of fat and fatlike substances play a role in cardiovascular disease, diabetes, cancer, and obesity. Fat is essential to our diet as protein and carbohydrates. Fat fuels our bodies with energy. Some vitamins require fat in order to dissolve into your bloodstream and provide nutrients. However, excess consumption of fat calories from eating leads to weight gain. Saturated fat is linked to high blood pressure, high cholesterol, and heart disease. Unsaturated fat, on the other hand, improves insulin sensitivity and reduces the risk of heart disease.

Besides carbs, proteins, and fats, other essential components for a balanced diet are fiber, vitamins, minerals, and water.

Fiber

Dietary fiber is classified as either soluble or insoluble. A mixture of both soluble and insoluble fiber is needed for good health. Soluble fiber changes how other nutrients are absorbed in the digestive system. Soluble fibers may reduce blood cholesterol and sugar. It helps your body improve blood glucose control, which can aid in reducing your risk for diabetes. Some foods can add to your diet to increase soluble fibers, such as black beans, lima beans, Pinto beans, kidney beans, tofu, avocados, and chickpeas. Insoluble fiber helps with digestion by speeding up the passage of food in the digestive system. Sources of insoluble fiber are oats, carrots, pistachios, nuts, cauliflowers, and green beans. The recommended daily intake of total fiber is 25 to 30 grams.

Flaxseed - Flaxseed is high in fiber and omega-3 fatty acids.

Incorporating flaxseeds in the diet will have intended benefits such as reduced cancer risk, lower cholesterol level, preventing cardiovascular disease, maintaining blood sugar, aiding in digestion, reducing inflammation, and lowering hypertension. Packed with protein, fiber, and omega-3 fatty acids, flax seeds can help lower the risk of certain cancers and maintain a healthy weight. Some of the notable benefits are: cancer prevention. Flaxseeds function as an antioxidant, effectively inhibiting the growth of breast, prostate, and skin cancer. These antioxidant properties play a crucial role in reducing damage caused by free radicals associated with cancer development.

Weight management: flax seeds have been shown to be beneficial in weight loss efforts. Numerous studies indicate that flax seeds can curb appetite and induce a feeling of fullness due to their high fiber content. The seed slows down the digestion process and activates hormones that reduce hunger cravings.

Cholesterol reduction: Studies have shown that a tablespoon (30 grams) of millet flaxseed per day can lower LDL cholesterol by 15%.

Vitamins and minerals:
Vitamins and minerals boost the immune system, support normal growth and development, and keep cells and organs doing their jobs. Vitamins are nutrients that help your body function. These are 13 essential vitamins the body needs: A, C, D, E, K, and B vitamins (thiamine, riboflavin, niacin, pantothenic acid, biotin, vitamin B6, vitamin B12, and folic acid). Each vitamin serves a specific purpose in the body. Vitamin A, for example, plays a role in vision, bone growth, reproduction, cell functions, and building immunity to infections. Vitamin C is necessary for the body to form collagen in bones and cartilage, muscle, and blood vessels. Vitamin C prevents colds. Vitamin D, also called 'sunshine vitamins', is essential for bone health, and its deficiency can make the bones soft and brittle, a condition called osteomalacia, resulting in body deformities and fractures. Vitamin D is important to prevent type 1 diabetes and hypertension. Vitamin D deficiency tends to occur more in areas such as Scandinavian countries, where sunshine is a precious commodity. Vitamin E is an antioxidant and plays a role in the formation of red blood cells, and helps the body use vitamin K. Vitamin K is essential for proper blood clotting. It may be vital for bone health also. The vitamin B group serves multiple functions. B6, folate, and B12 are essential for blood cell formation, and any deficiency can lead to anemia. Niacin (B3) contributes to the health of skin and nerves. Riboflavin (B2) is for body growth and the formation of red blood cells. Thiamine (B1) is for the integrity of the body cells and metabolism of carbohydrates, production of hormones, and cholesterol. These vitamins help your body convert the food you eat into energy. A lack of B12, folic acid, and B6 can cause anemia. Vitamin B6 is also vital for cardiac health. B12 influences nerve function and cognitive abilities.

Minerals are necessary for three reasons: building strong bones and teeth, controlling body fluids inside and outside cells, and turning the food you eat into energy. The important minerals for your body are calcium, iodine, iron, zinc and magnesium. Calcium is needed for strong bones, muscle and nerve function, and blood clotting. Milk, cheese, yogurt, salmon, and tofu provide calcium. Iodine helps the thyroid gland's function and normal growth. It is found in seafood, bread, and salt. Iron is needed for red blood cell function, helps move oxygen around the body, and makes energy. It's found in liver and red meat, salmon, legumes, green vegetables, eggs, etc. Zinc is helpful in wound healing, boosting immunity, and tissue repair. Zinc is found in oysters, seafood, meat, nuts, legumes, etc. Magnesium is essential for healthy muscles, nerves, bones, and blood sugar levels. It is possible to get all of the vitamins and minerals you need by eating a variety of healthy foods. But supplements can be useful for filling in gaps in your diet. It is estimated that two out of five Americans take vitamins and mineral supplements regularly, and nearly 50% of people over 50 years also take multivitamins.

WATER - Every day, you lose water through your breath, perspiration, urine and bowel movement. For your body to function properly, you must replenish its water supply. Water keeps every system in the body functioning properly. Water has many important jobs, such as carrying nutrients and oxygen in your cells, flushing bacteria from your bladder, aiding digestion, preventing constipation, normalizing blood pressure, cushioning joints, regulating body temperature, and maintaining electrolyte (sodium) balance. For healthy individuals, the average daily use of fluid for men is about 15.5 cups, for women, 11.5 cups. That means you need only four to six cups of plain water, depending on other fluid sources such as coffee, tea, fruits, and vegetables. Tea is the third most popular beverage in the U.S. after water and coffee. Green tea is the least processed and contains the most antioxidants. Herbal tea contains no caffeine and is not addictive. Ginger tea is used to curb nausea.

Healthy Diet – According to the World Health Organization (WHO), a healthy diet helps to protect against malnutrition in all its forms, as well as non-communicable diseases and conditions. However, increased production of processed food, rapid urbanization, and changing lifestyles have led to a shift in dietary patterns. People are consuming more food with high fats, free sugar, and salt/sodium, and people do not eat enough fruit, vegetables, and other dietary fiber, such as whole grains. Basic principles of what constitutes a healthy diet include the following:

- fruit, vegetables, legumes (lentil and beans), nuts, and whole grains like unprocessed maize, millet, oats.
- At least 400 grams (i.e., five portions) of fruit and vegetables per day, excluding potatoes and other starchy foods.
- Less than 30% of total energy intake from fats.

Unsaturated fats (found in fish, avocado, nuts, sunflower, soybean, canola and olive oil) are preferably to saturated fats (found in fatty meat, butter, palm and coconut oil, cream cheese, and lard) and trans-fat of all kinds, including produced trans-fat (found in baked and fried foods, and pre packed snacks and foods such as frozen pizza, pies, cakes, biscuit, wafers, and cooking oil and spreads). It is suggested that the intake of saturated fat be reduced to less than 10% of total energy intake and trans-fat to less than 1% of total energy intake.

- Less than 10% of total energy intake from free sugars, which is equivalent to 50 grams (or about 12 level tea spoons) for a person of healthy body weight consuming 2000 calories per day, but ideally, it's less than 5% of total energy intake for additional health benefits. Free sugars are all sugars added to food or drinks by manufacturers, cooks, or consumers, as well as sugars naturally present in honey, syrup, fruit juices, or concentrates.
- Less than 5 grams of salt (equivalent to about one teaspoon) per day. Salt should be iodized.

Practical Advice on Maintaining A Healthy Diet

Fruit and vegetables

Eating at least 400 grams or five portions of fruit and vegetables per day reduces the risk of non-communicable diseases (NCDs) and helps to ensure an adequate daily intake of dietary fiber. Fruit and vegetable intake can be improved by always including vegetables in meals, eating fresh fruits and raw vegetables as snacks.

Fat

Reducing the amount of total fat intake to less than 30% of total energy intake helps to prevent unhealthy weight gain in adults, and also lowers the risk of developing non-communicable diseases (NCDs). Fat intake, especially saturated fat and industrially produced trans-fat intake, can be reduced by steaming or boiling instead of frying when cooking; replacing butter and lard with oils rich in polyunsaturated fats, such as soybeans, canola. Corn, safflowers and sunflower oils, eating reduced-fat dairy foods and lean meats; limiting consumption of baked and fried foods and pre baked snacks like doughnuts, cakes, pies, cookies, biscuits and wafers that contain industrially produce trans-fat.

Salt, sodium, and potassium

An adult body needs around 1 to 2 gram of salt per day to function but not more than one teaspoon of salt (equivalent to 2300 mg of sodium per day). Most people consume much sodium through salt in the average 9 to 12 grams of salt per day and not enough potassium (less than 3.5 grams). High sodium intake and insufficient potassium intake contribute to high blood pressure, which in turn increases the risk of heart disease and stroke. Reducing salt intake to the recommended level of less than 5g per day could prevent (equals to 2000mg of sodium) could prevent 1.7 million deaths each year. Salt intake can be reduced by limiting the amount of salt and high-sodium condiments (e.g., soy sauce, fish sauce, and bouillon). When cooking and preparing foods; not having salt or high sauces on the table; limiting the consumption of salty snacks and choosing products with low sodium content.

Food Pyramid

The food pyramid is a representation of the optimum number of servings to be eaten each day from each of the five basic groups. Of carbohydrates, protein, dairy products, fruit and vegetables, and fat and sugar.

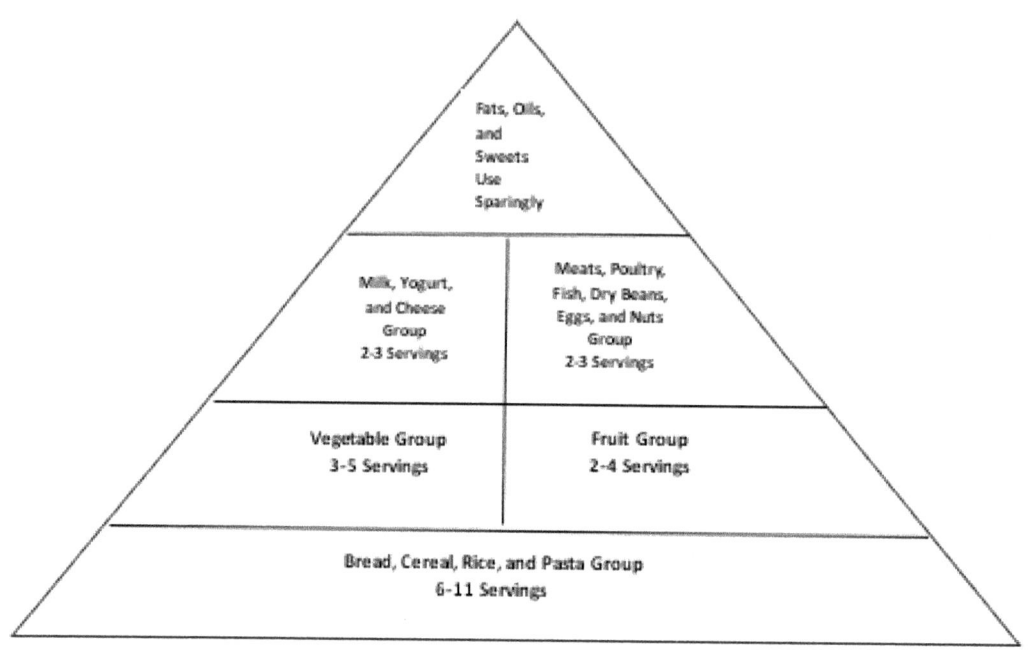

The food pyramid suggests what foods should be consumed most at the bottom of the pyramid. The amount that should be eaten least is found at the top of the pyramid. The food pyramid was initially proposed by Sweden. In recent times food pyramid has been replaced by the food diet plate.

Diet Plate

On this plate, you eat three meals and two snacks a day. The healthy eating plate is a guide for creating a healthy, balanced meal.

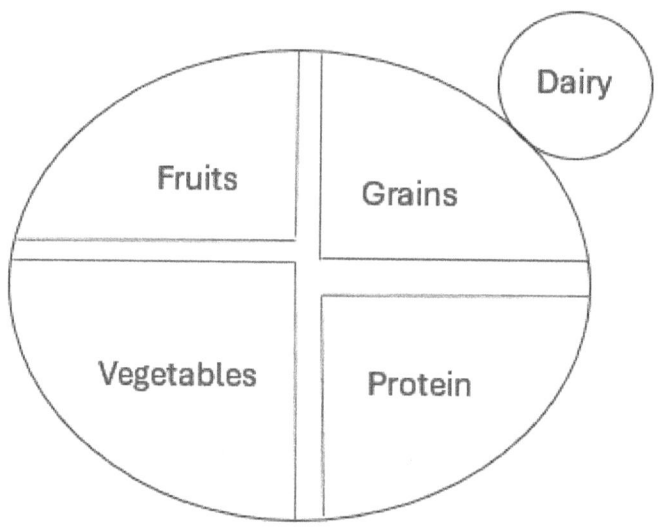

Make most of your meal vegetables and fruits-1/2 of your plate. Aim for color and variety, and remember that potatoes don't count as vegetables in the healthy eating plate because of their negative impact on blood sugar. 1/4 of your plate should be whole wheat, barley, berries, quinoa, oats, brown rice, and food made with them. 1/4 of your plate consists of protein power, like fish, poultry, beans, and nuts. Limit red meat, and avoid processed meats such as bacon and sausage. Healthy plant oils in moderation, like olive oil, canola oil, corn oil, and sunflower oil. Avoid partially hydrogenated oils. Drink water, coffee, or tea. Skip sugar drinks, limit milk and dairy products to one or two servings per day, and limit juice to a small glass per day.

Quick High Energy Snacks

Going too long without eating makes you feel tired, cranky, and spaced out. Small healthy snacks or mini meals that include protein and carbohydrates will help keep your energy level high throughout the day. Here is a suggested list of healthy snacks:

- Slice an apple and peanut butter (one tablespoon)
- Turkey 2 slices and tomato on whole wheat bread
- low-fat cottage cheese (1/2 a cup) and one slice of pear
- almonds (1/2 a cup) and dried apricots
- low-fat yogurt and fruit smoothie
- hummus (quarter cup) and slice red bell pepper (1 cup)
- slice of cheese (1 1/2 oz) and whole grain cracker (5)
- have a peanut butter and banana sandwich
- tablespoon of peanut butter, one piece of whole grain bread

Maintaining Optimum Health Through Meat Alternatives

According to many scientific studies, healthy non-meat diets can offer appropriate nutrition while avoiding some of the health hazards linked to excessive consumption of animal foods. A non-meat diet includes vegetarians and a vegan diet. The difference between a vegan diet and a vegetarian diet is that a vegan diet excludes a broad range of foods from animals. Both vegetarian and vegan diets exclude meat, poultry, and fish. In addition, a vegan diet also avoids eggs and dairy products such as milk, yogurt, cheese, and butter.

A vegan diet is becoming popular with some professional athletes, like tennis superstar Venus Williams and environmental activist Greta Thunberg, and others. The number of people in the US who identify themselves as vegan increased to 6% up from 1% in 2014. Compared to animal-based foods, plant-based foods tend to have more fiber, phytonutrients, and antioxidants, while having less saturated fat and cholesterol. A healthy vegan diet consists of minimal processed plant-based food that minimizes the use of refined ingredients, such as oils, white sugar, and white flour. Also, due to a low amount of dietary cholesterol, a healthy vegan diet can help to lower cholesterol levels and reduce the risk of heart disease. A healthy vegan diet can also lower blood pressure, reduce the risk of type 2 diabetes, and is associated with a lower risk of certain types of cancer, such as breast and prostate cancer.

Research studies also demonstrate that vegan diets can be quite healthy, particularly in terms of lower body mass index (BMI), lower heart disease risk, and lower prevalence of hypertension. It is important to know that vegan diets can have nutrient deficiencies like iodine, vitamin B12, omega-3, calcium, zinc, iron, magnesium, and high-quality protein. Fortified foods and supplements are the only proven, reliable source for vegans. However, there are global benefits of vegan diets. That topic will be covered under global Wellness.

Health Care In The United States

The United States ranks last overall in the healthcare outcome domain, among the top ten industrialized countries. U.S. performance is lowest among the top advanced countries, including having the highest infant mortality rate of 5.7 deaths per 100,000 live births. Despite having the most expensive health care system, the U.S. ranks last overall compared with six other industrialized countries -Australia, Canada, Germany, the Netherlands, New Zealand, and the United Kingdom in the measures of quality, efficiency, access to care, equity, and ability to lead a healthy life. Some high-income nations get more for their health dollars than the U.S. does.

American fraud, overcharging, and a lack of emphasis on preventive care are some of the main reasons for the ineffective health care system in the U.S. The General Accounting Office estimates that healthcare fraud, waste, and abuse may account for as much as 10 percent of all healthcare expenditures. That is a billion dollars a week. Overcharging is the dark side of health care consolidation. Dr. Ernesto Pretio Jr., professor of clinical anesthesiology in Coral Cables, Florida, stated as a guest column in the Orlando Sentinel newspaper that private equity firms and large, well-funded health care corporations are acquiring independent physician practices, nursing homes, and other physician groups, then continuing to deliver the same medical services, but charging higher fees. To give a specific example, the cost of colonoscopy or esophagus duodenoscopy (EGD) rose from $527 to $2679 under the new takeover management. Procedures performed and the physician who performed the procedure are the same, but under new management, and costs have increased significantly.

I had come across a physician in a social setting. She informed me that her medical practice has been taken over by a large hospital corporation, and she was given hundreds of thousands of dollars for switching to this new hospital corporation. How is the hospital going to recover the money? It is simple by overcharging the patent. It was reported that a big cardiology group was not only overcharging, but also billing insurance incorrectly for stent procedures in the arteries. Finally, the group settled the claims by paying millions of dollars. This kind of thing causes the medical costs to skyrocket, and more and more people are neglecting their health care because they cannot afford to see a doctor, get a test, or even undergo a medical treatment. One in 11 American rely on the community health care center. The report says that many centers are short-staffed. The article in the newspaper reported that funding needs to be increased by billions of dollars in community health centers as the number of patients is increasing and the health centers can't keep up with the greater demand and the needs of community patients. Health care spending, both per person and as a share of GDP, continues to be far higher in the U.S. than in other high-income countries, yet the U.S. is the only country that doesn't have universal health coverage.

Health Diseases in the United States

Maintaining good health and living a full life involves living a life free of disease. Much attention has been paid in recent years to life expectancy in the U.S., which remains lower than in many other industrialized nations that spend less on health care. Data suggesting 79% of adults 60 and older have two or more chronic illnesses, such as diabetes, heart disease and high blood pressure- and more than half of young adults reporting at least one chronic condition, health experts are turning their focus not just how long people manage to stay alive but the number of years they expect to do so free of disease. That is what's called health span, like U.S. life span; these, too, have been shrinking.

Health span means living better, not just longer. The steps needed to extend a person's health span are likely to extend their life span as well. The factors that help prevent the onset of disease are also highly related to preventing your death from those diseases. These factors include not smoking, staying active, getting enough sleep, following a healthy eating pattern, maintaining a healthy weight, and controlling cholesterol, blood pressure, and blood glucose.

The ten leading causes of death in the U.S. are heart disease, cancer, accidents, chronic lower respiratory diseases, Alzheimer's disease, diabetes, influenza and pneumonia, kidney disease, and suicide. Two main causes of death in the U.S. and the world are heart disease and cancer; therefore, these diseases will be covered in more detail.

Ten leading causes of death in the United States

Heart Disease- Heart disease is the number one cause of death in the U.S. The Number of deaths per year is 635,260. Percent of deaths: 23.1 percent. Heart disease is more common among men, people who smoke, people who are overweight or obese, people with a family history of heart disease or heart attack, and people who are over age 55. Causes of heart disease are arrhythmias (irregular heartbeat), coronary artery disease (blocked arteries), and heart defects.

Tips for prevention

Lifestyle changes, such as quitting smoking, eating a healthy diet, exercising at least 30 minutes per day, and checking vitamin levels with a micronutrient test. This micronutrient test checks for vitamin B12, D, E, C, copper, and selenium. Heart disease is the leading cause of death for both men and women in the United States. Coronary artery disease (CAD)is one of the major diseases of the heart. CAD is the narrowing or blockage of the coronary arteries caused by atherosclerosis. Atherosclerosis occurs due to cholesterol and plaque buildup in the walls of arteries. Plaque buildup can restrict blood flow to the heart muscle and deprive the heart of the oxygen and nutrients it needs. Besides high cholesterol, damage to the coronary arteries may be caused by diabetes, high blood pressure (B.P.), a sedentary lifestyle, and smoking. For a sedentary lifestyle, physical activity is important (look under the exercise section). A lot of stress may damage the arteries and worsen the risk factor for CAD (look under the mental/ emotional section). Adequate sleep is also necessary to relieve stress (see under sleep). Risk factors occur together. One risk factor may trigger another. Other risk factors for CAD may include breathing pauses during sleep (obstructive sleep apnea). It can cause a sudden drop in blood oxygen levels. It may increase blood pressure. High C-reactive protein causes inflammation in the body. As coronary arteries narrow, the level of C-reactive protein in the blood goes up. A high level of triglycerides may also increase the risk of CAD. Complications of CAD can lead to angina (chest pain). Heart disease can happen if a cholesterol plaque breaks open and causes a blood clot to form. A clot can block the blood flow and thus damage the heart muscle.

Preventive measures to improve heart health include quitting smoking, controlling high blood pressure, exercising often, maintaining a healthy weight, eating a low-fat, low-salt diet that is rich in fruits, vegetables, and whole grains, and reducing and mange stress.

Cancer- Cancer is the second leading cause of death in the U.S. The Number of deaths per year is 598,038. The percent of total depth is 21.7%. Risk factors include people at a certain age, people who use tobacco and alcohol, people exposed to radiation and lots of sunlight, people with chronic inflammation, people who are obese, and people with a family history of disease. Causes of cancer are the result of rapid and uncontrolled cell growth in your body. A normal cell of growth modifies and divides in a controlled manner. Sometimes those instructions become scrambled. When this happens, the cells begin to divide at an uncontrollable rate. This can develop into cancer.

Tips for Prevention

Certain behaviors have been linked to an increased cancer risk, like smoking. Good changes in behavior include maintaining a healthy weight, eating a balanced diet, exercising regularly, quitting smoking and drinking in moderation, avoiding direct exposure to the sun for extended periods of time, not using tanning beds, having regular cancer screenings, including skin checkups, mammograms, prostate exams, etc.

In the United States, researchers estimate that as many as 42% of cancer cases and 45% of cancer deaths could be prevented if people adopted effective risk reduction measures as stated above. In addition, the human papillomavirus (HPV)vaccine can prevent up to 90% of cancers triggered by HPV infections.

The most common cancers are breast cancer in women, cervical cancer, colorectal cancer, lung cancer primarily due to smoking, ovarian cancer, prostate cancer in men, and skin cancer. More people in the U.S. die from lung cancer than from any other type of cancer. Many are heavy smokers. Prostate cancer is the second most commonly diagnosed cancer and the second leading cause of cancer death in men. Breast cancer represents 30% of all newly diagnosed cancers in women. One in every three Americans will develop some form of malignancy during his or her lifetime. Scientists at Harvard School of Public Health estimate that up to 75% of American Cancer deaths can be prevented. The 10 commandments of cancer prevention are:

1. Avoid tobacco in all forms, including secondhand smoke
2. Eat properly. Reduce your consumption of saturated fat and red meat
3. Exercise regularly
4. Stay lean. Obesity increases the risk of many forms of cancer
5. Limit yourself to an average of one alcoholic drink a day. Excessive drinking increases the risk of cancer of the mouth.
6. Avoid excessive exposure to radiation
7. Avoid exposure to industrial and environmental toxins such as asbestos. Benzene, aromatic amines, and polychlorinated biphenyls (PCBs).
8. Avoid infections that contribute to cancer, including the hepatitis virus, HIV, and HPV
9. Make quality sleep properly
10. Get enough vitamin D. Vitamin D may help reduce the risk of prostate cancer and colon cancer

Accidents - (Unintended injuries) Number of deaths per year: 161,374, percentage of total deaths: 5.9%, more common among men, people aged up to 44 years, and people with risky jobs. Causes of Death -Accidents lead to more than 28 million emergency room visits each year. Three leading causes of accident-related death are unintended falls, motor vehicle traffic deaths, and unintentional poisoning deaths.

Unattended injuries may be the result of carelessness. Be aware of your surroundings. Take all precautions to prevent accidents or injuries. If you hurt yourself, seek emergency medical treatment to prevent serious complications.

Chronic lower respiratory diseases- Number of deaths per year: 154,596,

percentage of total deaths: 5.1%. Most common among women, people over 65, people with a history of smoking or exposure to secondhand smoke, people with a history of asthma, individuals, and lower-income households. This group of diseases includes chronic obstructive pulmonary disease (COPD), emphysema, asthma, and pulmonary hypertension. Each of these conditions or diseases prevents your lungs from working properly. They can also cause scarring and damage to the lung tissues.

Tips For Prevention

Tobacco and secondhand smoke exposure are the primary factors in the development of these diseases. Quit smoking, limit your exposure to others' smoke to reduce your risk.

Stroke- Number of deaths per year: 142,142. The percentage of total deaths is 5.1%. Most

common among men, women using birth control, people with diabetes, people with B.P., people with heart disease, and people who smoke. Causes of Stroke- A stroke occurs when the blood flow to your brain is cut off without oxygen. Your brain cells begin to die in a matter of minutes. Blood flow can be stopped because of a blocked artery and bleeding in the brain. These bleedings may be from an aneurysm or a broken blood vessel.

Tips for Prevention

lifestyle changes, maintain a healthy weight, exercise more and eat healthy, manage B.P., stop smoking, drink in moderation, manage sugar level and diabetes, and treat underlying heart defects and diseases.

Alzheimer's Disease- Number of deaths per year: 116,103. Percent of

total deaths: 4.23% most common among people over 65 (the risk for Alzheimer's doubles every five years), and people with a family history of the disease. Causes of Alzheimer's Disease- it can be a combination of a person's genes, lifestyle, and environment. Some of the changes occur before the first symptoms appear.

Tips for prevention

While you cannot control your age or genetics, which are two of the most common risk factors for the disease, you can control lifestyle factors that may decrease your risk for it. Exercise on a regular basis, eat a diet filled with fruit and vegetables, healthy treats, and monitor any other chronic disease. Keep your brain active with stimulating tasks like puzzles and reading.

Diabetes- Number of deaths per year: 80,058. The percentage of total deaths is 2.9. Type 1 diabetes is more common among people with a family history of the disease, or a specific gene that increases the risk, children and young adults, and people living in climates farther away from the equator. Type 2 diabetes is more common among people who are overweight or obese, adults over 45, and people who have a family history of diabetes. Causes of diabetes- Type 1 diabetes occurs when your pancreas cannot produce enough insulin. Type 2 diabetes occurs when your body becomes resistant to insulin or does not make enough of it to control your blood sugar levels.

Tips for prevention-

You can't prevent type 1 diabetes. However, you may prevent type 2 diabetes with several lifestyle changes like the following: maintain a healthy weight, exercise for at least 30 minutes five days a week, eat a healthy diet with plenty of fruits, vegetables, whole grains, and lean protein, and have a regular blood sugar checkup if you have a family history of the disease.

Influenza and Pneumonia- number of deaths per year: 51,537. The percentage of the total deaths is 1.88%. Most common among children, the elderly, and people with chronic health conditions. Causes of influenza and pneumonia- Influenza (the flu) is a highly contagious viral infection. It is very common during the winter season. Pneumonia is an infection and inflammation of the lungs. The flu is one of the leading causes of pneumonia.

Tips for prevention

People in the high-risk category should get a flu vaccine. Anyone concerned about it should get one too. To prevent the spread of the flu, be sure to wash your hands well and avoid people who are sick. Likewise, the pneumonia vaccine is available for people at high risk of developing the infection.

Kidney disease- Number of deaths per year: 50,004. The percentage of total deaths is 1.8%. More common among people with other chronic conditions, including diabetes, high blood pressure, and recurring kidney infection, people who smoke, people who are overweight or obese, and people with a family history of kidney disease. Kidney disease refers to three main conditions: nephritis (kidney inflammation), nephrotic syndrome, and nephrosis. Nephrotic syndrome produces a high level of protein in your urine; nephrosis leads to kidney failure as a result of damage to the kidneys from either physical or chemical changes.

Tips For Prevention

Eat a low-sodium diet, stop smoking and drinking, and lose weight if overweight or obese.

Suicide- Number of deaths per year: 44,905, percentage of total deaths: 1.6%. The most common among men, people with injuries, people who have attempted suicide, have a history of depression and other mental health conditions, misuse of alcohol and drugs, and a history of self-harm injuries. Self-harm injuries- Almost 50,000 people are treated in emergency rooms each year for self-inflicted injuries.

Tips For Prevention

Find a support system of family and friends, and in some cases, medical or hospital treatments. Contact the suicide prevention hotline 800-273-8255, offering 24/7 support. Seek mental health services. This topic is covered in more detail under the mental/emotional health section.

The top causes of death globally are covered under global Wellness.

Strengthening Your Defense Against Diseases

To maintain good health, it is important to know certain parameters about good health, what we call the normal range of values. Knowing the numbers, you can take steps to improve your health and reduce the risk of heart disease, diabetes, and other illnesses.

Body Mass Index (BMI) - your body mass index (BMI) measures your weight in relation to your height and is a universally accepted index for the evaluation of body obesity. BMI correlates highly with body fat in most people. To find your BMI risk level, weigh and measure yourself wearing very little clothing and no shoes. Find your height in inches and weight in pounds.

BMI Calculations: weight divided by height in inches squared multiplied by 703. Example, if weight is 150 lbs. and height is 5'5" (65"). Calculation is

150 / (65) squared x 703 = 24.96. BMI Values key

- Less than 18.5 - underweight
- 18.5 – 24.9 - Healthy
- 25-29.9 - Overweight
- 30 or higher - Obese
- 40 or higher - Extreme Obesity

There are other ways to assess excess body fat besides BMI. Other methods include skin fold thickness measurement with calipers.

Health consequences of obesity for adults- People who have obesity are at increased risk of many diseases and health conditions, including high blood pressure(hypertension), high LDL cholesterol or low HDL cholesterol, high levels are triglycerides, type 2 diabetes, coronary heart disease (CHD) osteoarthritis (a breaking down of cartilage and bone within a joint), sleep apnea or breathing problems, chronic inflammation, some cancer, (endometrial, breast, colon, kidney and liver) body pain and difficulties with physical faculty.

Weight control tips per the American Heart Association

You can teach your body to burn calories. Just become more physically active. You should not lose weight too fast. One-half to one pound a week is best. Regular physical activity is one of the best predictors of who will lose weight and keep it off. Quick weight loss diets don't work. Body mass index (BMI) is a great indicator of your height-to-weight ratio.

Choose lean cuts of meat in small portions or low-fat dairy foods.

Satisfy your hunger with fresh fruits, vegetables, cereals, whole-grain bread, and dried beans. These have more nutrients than sugar, like soft drinks and candy. A low-carb diet is used for weight loss. Some low-carb diets may have benefits beyond weight loss, such as lowering your risk of type 2 diabetes and metabolic syndrome. A low-carb diet is meant to cause the body to burn stored fat for energy, which leads to weight loss. A daily limit of 0.7 to 2 ounces (20 to 57 grams) of carbohydrates is typically associated with a low-carb diet. For most people, 100 to 150 grams of carbohydrates is safe when trying to lose weight. Most people can lose weight if they limit calories and boost their physical activity. To lose 1 to 5 pounds a week, you need to eat 500 to 750 fewer calories each day.

Prepare your food without added fat- Try these cooking methods: roast, bake, sauté, broil, grill, steam, poach, stir-fry, and microwave—season with herbs, wine, and fruit juices instead of fats.

Eat less, more often, to keep the hunger away. Plan ahead and avoid skipping meals.

Listen to your hunger signals-when you want to eat something, decide if you are truly feeling hunger signals or if you are bored, lonely, sad, or feeling some other emotion or mood. If you are not physically hungry, do something else. If you are truly hungry, eat a healthy meal or snack.

Physical Activity

Start slowly. See your doctor before you begin a fairly vigorous program if you are middle-aged or older and have been inactive for several years, or have a medical condition. Start by walking at a comfortable pace for 15 minutes, 365 days a week. Take the stairs and park farther away from your destination. Ride bikes with your family, walk your dog, and enjoy outdoor games. Develop active pastimes and hobbies, such as gardening or hiking. Choose an activity you enjoy and that will be easy for you to do often. Biking, walking, jogging, swimming, rowing, and cross-country skiing are excellent fat-burning workouts up to 30-60 minutes at a time, 3-5 times per week. A good way to burn excess fat is to exercise at a moderate pace for a longer time and to do it regularly.

Blood Pressure

Blood pressure is the force of blood pushing against the walls of arteries as the heart pumps blood. When a health care professional measures your blood pressure, they use a blood pressure cuff around your arm that tightens and then gradually loosens. The results are given in two numbers. The first number, called systolic blood pressure, is the pressure caused by your heart contracting and pushing out blood. The second number, called diastolic blood pressure, is the pressure when your heart relaxes and fills with blood. A blood pressure reading is given as the systolic blood pressure number over the diastolic blood pressure number. Low blood pressure, or hypotension, is a systolic blood pressure lower than 90 or a diastolic blood pressure lower than 60. If you have low blood pressure, you may feel lightheaded, weak, dizzy, or even faint. It can be caused by not getting enough fluids, blood loss due to some medical condition, or medication, including those prescribed for high blood pressure. Normal blood pressure for most adults is defined as a systolic pressure of less than 120 and a diastolic pressure of less than 80 mmHg. The researchers found the following breakdown by age, sex, and race or ethnicity in the blood pressure.

Blood Pressure by Age

	Men	Women
18-35	119/70 mmHg	110/68 mmHg
40-50	124/77 mmHg	122/74 mmHg
60+ years	133/69 mmHg	139/68 mmHg

Blood Pressure by Race/ Ethnicity

White	122/71 mmHg
Black	127/73 mmHg
Mexican American	123/70 mmHg

Stages of High Blood Pressure

	Systolic	Diastolic
Elevated	120-129 mmHg	less than 80 mmHg
Stage 1 Hypertension	130/139mmHg	80-89 mmHg
Stage 2 Hypertension	140 mmHg and up	90 mmHg and up
Hypertension Crisis	180 mmHg and up	120 mmHg and up

180/120 is a sharp increase in blood pressure, which may cause a stroke

A constant rise in your blood pressure over time comes with an increased risk to your health. Your health care provider is likely to respond in three ways:

Elevated: You are likely to develop hypertension unless you take steps to control it. These may include lifestyle changes such as eating a heart-healthy diet, getting more exercise, and quitting smoking.

Stage 1 hypertension: Your health care provider will probably recommend lifestyle changes. They may also prescribe medication, depending on your risk for cardiovascular disease, heart attack, or stroke.

Stage 2 hypertension: Your health care provider will likely prescribe both medication and lifestyle changes to lower your blood pressure.

Hypertension crises: Seek medical attention right away if your blood pressure is high. You could experience a heart attack, stroke, or something else that can damage your organs or threaten your life.

Risk factors for high blood pressure include:

Little or no exercise- People who do not exercise regularly are at greater risk of hypertension and heart disease.

Unhealthy diet -Diets that are higher in salt, sugar, saturated fat, and trans- fat are linked to high blood pressure and increased risk of cardiovascular disease.

Obesity – Being overweight or obese makes your heart work harder to move blood and oxygen through your body.

Suggestions for controlling blood pressure

You can lower your blood pressure by changing your day-to-day habits and by taking medication if needed. Treatment requires evaluations and discussions with your doctor, especially if you have other medical conditions such as diabetes. Lifestyle changes you can make to help prevent and lower high blood pressure are:

- Aim for a healthy weight. Being overweight adds to your risk of high blood pressure.
- Exercise- Moderate activity, such as walking or swimming, can lower high blood pressure.
- Set goals so you can safely work your way up to at least 150 minutes per week.
- Eat a heart-healthy diet- A balanced diet of vegetables, fruit, grains, protein, and dairy.
- Cut down on salt- As you get older, the body and blood pressure become more sensitive to salt(sodium), which is added to many foods during processing or preparation. Limiting the amount of salt you consume may help.

- Drink less alcohol. Drinking alcohol can affect your blood pressure. For those who drink, men should have no more than two drinks a day and women no more than one a day to lower their risk of high blood pressure.

- Don't smoke- Smoking increases your risk for high blood pressure, heart disease, stroke, and other health problems. If you smoke, quit.

- Get a good night's sleep- Tell your doctor if you have sleep apnea. Treating sleep apnea and getting a good night's sleep can help lower your blood pressure.

- Manage stress- Coping with problems and reducing stress can help lower blood pressure.

Diet and Cholesterol

Cholesterol is an odorless, white, waxy powder. Cholesterol is a compound that is similar to fat. It is needed by the body to form the outside barrier of cells (membrane). It can be made both by the liver in the body and consumed through sources in the diet. Cholesterol can't dissolve in your blood, so it travels to and from cells on carriers, called lipoproteins. Two types of lipoprotein are low-density (LDL) and high-density lipoprotein. High levels of cholesterol in the blood are associated with damaged arteries and contribute to heart disease. Specifically, high LDL and low levels of HDL in the blood increase the risk of heart disease. Lipoproteins are particles made up of lipids (fats) and proteins that carry fats through your bloodstream. Fats, because of their structure, can't move through your blood on their own. So, lipoproteins serve as a vehicle that carries fats to various cells in your body. LDL particles contain a large amount of cholesterol and a smaller amount of protein. Excess LDL cholesterol contributes to plaque buildup (atherosclerosis) in your arteries. This plaque buildup may lead to coronary heart disease, cerebrovascular disease, peripheral disease, and aortic aneurysm. HDL, on the other hand, carries cholesterol away from cells to your liver, where it is broken down. It is often called good cholesterol because it helps remove cholesterol. Having a high HDL cholesterol level lowers the chances of heart disease.

Complications from high cholesterol- When you have a plaque buildup from high LDL and low HDL, it increases your risk of other health conditions and complications, including-

- Hardening of your arteries and high blood pressure. Plaque causes your arteries to become narrower, harder, and less flexible. This means your heart has to strain to pump blood through them, causing high blood pressure.
- Coronary artery disease (CAD) and angina (chest pain)- Over time, hardened and narrow arteries keep a slow blood flow from reaching your heart, so it does not get the oxygen it needs.
- Heart attack- If plaque ruptures or breaks open, a blood clot can form and block the flow of blood and oxygen to your heart, causing a heart attack.
- Stoke- If the arteries that carry blood and oxygen to your brain become narrow or blocked, then parts of your brain can't get the blood and oxygen they need, causing a stroke.
- Peripheral vascular disease (PAD)- Plaque buildup or hardened, narrowed arteries can happen in other areas of your body, like your legs. Having high cholesterol can also increase your risk of type 2 diabetes.

Know your Numbers

Your total cholesterol is a combination of LDL+HDL+20% of your triglycerides. A normal cholesterol level should be less than 200 mg/dl. LDL levels above 100 mg/dl raise your risk of cardiovascular disease. Health care providers use the following categories to describe your LDL

Normal below 100 mg/dl

Near optimum 100-120 mg/dl

Borderline high 130-159 mg/dl

Very high 190-mg/dl or higher

Health care providers check your cholesterol through a simple blood test called a lipid panel. Generally, a health care provider encourages high HDL cholesterol levels (ideally above 60) and lower LDL cholesterol levels to reduce your cardiovascular disease risk.

Causes of high LDL cholesterol

Many factors can raise your LDL levels. The factors you have some control over include: What you eat- Foods like fatty meats, full-fat dairy products, bakery, and fast food are harmful for your cholesterol level. That is because they contain high amounts of saturated fat and, in some cases, trans-fat. These two types of fat raise your LDL Cholesterol.

Your body weight- Having body weight/obesity can raise your LDL cholesterol.

Smoking- or using tobacco products. Tobacco use lowers your HDL level and increases LDL levels.

Foods that cause LDL cholesterol are bakery items like doughnuts, cookies, and cake. Full-fat dairy products like whole milk, cheese, and butter, red meats, like steak, ribs, pork chips, and ground beef, processed meats like bacon, hot dogs, and sausage, and fried foods, like French fries and fried chicken.

Lowering your LDL cholesterol- Here are some of the changes you can make

Follow a heart-healthy diet like healthy fats (from sources like olive oil and nuts).

Avoid tobacco use

Get more exercise-Aim for 30 minutes of aerobic exercise per day, at least 5 days a week.

Keep a healthy weight for you.

Find strategies to lower your stress- follow techniques like yoga and deep breathing exercises to manage stress.

Foods that can lower your LDL cholesterol are black beans, lima beans, navy beans, kidney beans, Tofu, avocado, chick peas, broccoli, and apples. A diet to lower LDL (bad) cholesterol and increase HDL (good) cholesterol can include:

Healthy Fats- Foods like avocado, nuts, seeds, olives, plant or seed oil, and fish contain healthy fats that can increase HDL cholesterol. Healthy fats include omega-3 fatty acids, monounsaturated fats, and polyunsaturated fats. Some examples of oily fish that are high in omega-3 fatty acids include salmon, mackerel, seabass, oysters, sardines, and tuna.

High-Fiber foods- Foods like vegetables, fruits, whole grains, legumes, nuts, and seeds contain dietary fiber, especially soluble fiber, which can reduce LDL cholesterol. Soluble fiber can also increase HDL cholesterol levels by reducing the amount of cholesterol absorbed into the bloodstream. Some examples of fiber-rich foods include oat bran, whole oats, beans, peas, flaxseed, and oatmeal.

Plant Protein- Eating more protein from plant sources, like soy, tofu, and soy protein shakes. Vegetables like tomatoes contain lycopene, a substance that can reduce LDL production, help break down cholesterol, so it can be removed from the body.

Nuts- Regular consumption of tree nuts like walnuts and almonds is tied to lower levels of total cholesterol, LDL cholesterol, and triglycerides.

Legumes- Half a cup serving of legumes, including beans, peanuts, lentils, and peas, could lower your LDL cholesterol. Like oats, beans are packed with soluble fiber that sweeps cholesterol out of the bloodstream.

Seeds- like whole grains, seeds are rich in fiber, which binds to bad cholesterol and drives it out of the body. Chia seeds and flax seeds are especially good to add to your diet.

Fruits- Many fruits are high in fiber and antioxidants, which can lower cholesterol and improve heart health. Some fruits can help lower cholesterol, including apples, bananas, pears, and prunes, which contain pectin, a type of soluble fiber, to lower LDL. Berries like blackberries, blueberries, and strawberries are high in soluble fiber and low in sugar.

Vegetables- Dark leafy greens, such as kale and spinach, contain lutein and carotenoids, which are linked to a lower risk of cholesterol and a lower risk of heart disease. Other vegetables that also lower cholesterol are brussels sprouts, broccoli, cauliflower, zucchini, eggplant, and tomatoes. Tomatoes contain lycopene, a substance that can reduce LDL production and help break down cholesterol so it can be removed from the body.

You can also try cooking with healthy oils like olive oil in small amounts, baking, broiling, or steaming your food instead of frying it.

Triglyceride and LDL

Triglycerides are fat molecules that help in metabolism and moving other fats around the body. Like cholesterol, high levels of triglyceride in the blood have been linked to heart disease. When your LDL cholesterol and triglycerides are too high and /or your HDL is too low, it can cause plaque build-up in the walls of your arteries. This is called atherosclerosis. When you have plaque build-up, your risk of other health conditions and complications, such as coronary heart disease (CHD) and angina (chest pain), increases over time. If plaque ruptures or breaks open, a blood clot can form and block the flow of blood and oxygen to your heart, causing a heart attack. If the arteries that carry blood and oxygen to your brain become narrow or blocked, then parts of your brain can't get the blood or oxygen they need, which can cause a stroke. Plaque build-up or hardened arteries can happen in other organs of your body, like your legs, contributing to peripheral artery disease (PAD).

Sugar (Glucose)

Sugar is a carbohydrates that provide the body with energy, so it has an important role in nutrition. The problem people have with sugar is that they often consume too much of the wrong kind. Natural sugars are found in whole fruits, vegetables, milk products, and grains. Fruit and some vegetables contain a form of sugar, called fructose, glucose, and sucrose, while milk contains lactose, and grains contain maltose. Current guidelines recommend you eat about two cups of fruit and two to three cups of vegetables per day, six ounces of whole grains like brown rice, oats, and quinoa. Fruits, vegetables, and grains also contain fiber, phytochemicals, antioxidants, and various vitamins and minerals you need for optimal health. In comparison, refined sugar is added to food products to improve taste. Refined sugar comes from cane, sugar beets, and corn, which are processed to isolate sugar. The top food sources of added refined sugar include soft drinks, fruit-flavored drinks, flavored yogurt, cereals, cookies, and cake.

In both adults and children, the intake of free sugars should be reduced to less than 10% of total energy intake. A reduction of less than 5% of total energy intake would provide additional health benefits. Consuming free sugar increases the risk of tooth decay. Excess calories from foods and drinks in free sugars also contribute to unhealthy weight gain, which can lead to overweight and obesity. Free sugars influence blood pressure and serum lipids, and a reduction in free sugar intake reduces risk factors for cardiovascular diseases. Sugar intake can be reduced by limiting the consumption of foods and drinks containing high amounts of sugar, such as sugary snacks, candies, and sugar-sweetened beverages, and eating fresh fruits and raw vegetables instead of sugary snacks.

Sugar comes from food and your liver, and goes to your bloodstream. Your cells use sugar for energy. Insulin keeps sugar from your blood into your cells. Insulin is a hormone made in your pancreas. It acts as a key and attaches to cells so they open often and let sugar inside. Without the right amount of insulin, there is too much sugar in your blood. This causes damage to your blood vessels and nerves. With type 1 diabetes, your body does not make enough insulin. With Type 2 diabetes, your body doesn't make enough insulin or it doesn't use insulin like it should. When you were first diagnosed with diabetes, you may have had symptoms of high blood sugar. Once you begin treatment, you will need to watch out for low blood sugar as well. Work with your doctor to learn how to prevent high and lows, and how to recognize and treat them.

Fasting Blood Sugar and HbA1c

Normal fasting blood sugar is 99mg/dl or below. Pre-diabetes 100-125. Diabetes 126 or higher. Your post-prandial blood sugar (blood sugar measured two hours after the meal) should be less than 200. Ideally, less than 140. HbA1c or glycated hemoglobin in the non-diabetes range is below 5.7%. Anyone with an HbA1c value of less than 5.7 to 6.4 is considered to be prediabetic. An HbA1C of 6.5% or higher is consistent with Diabetes Mellitus (DM). HbA1c represents the average plasma glucose concentration over a prolonged period of time. Hence, it is useful in deciding the control of DM in a patient.

The hemoglobin A1C (glycated hemoglobin, Hb A1C) test is used to evaluate a person's level of glucose control. The test showed an indication of blood sugar level over the past 90 days.

The test can also be used to diagnose diabetes. Less than half of these newly diagnosed get the A1C to the target goal of 7%. About 282,000 people with diabetes go to the ER for low blood sugar levels each year. Your doctor may give the results of your A1C test in a number that matches the blood sugar reading you are used to seeing. This number is called eAG, or average glucose. An A1C of 7% is equal to an eAG of 154mg/dl. See the chart below.

A1C	6%	7%	8%	9%	10%	11%	12%
Converts to							
eAG mg/dl	126	154	183	212	240	269	298

High Blood Sugar

High blood sugar is called hyperglycemia. You usually won't notice symptoms until your blood sugar is over 200 mg/dl (milligram per deciliter). Symptoms include feeling thirsty, urinating more often, blurred vision, feeling tired, and headaches. Making changes to your diet and exercising more could help.

Low Blood Sugar

Low blood sugar is called hypoglycemia. It usually means your blood sugar is less than 70mg/dl. Symptoms often come on quickly and may include shakiness, confusion, hunger, sweating or chills, lightheadedness or dizziness, blurred vision, feeling nervous or anxious, feeling irritable or impatient, rapid heartbeat, and feeling sleepy.

Everyone reacts differently to low blood sugar, so it is important to learn to watch for the usual signs you experience. If you think your blood sugar is low, follow these medical guidelines:

Eat or drink 15 to 20 grams of glucose or simple carbohydrates. Examples include glucose tablets, ¼ cup of juice, regular soda, or hard candy. If you can't get your blood sugar to return to a normal range, call your doctor or go to the emergency room. Severe low blood sugar can cause serious complications like coma or passing out.

Causes of high blood sugar and low blood sugar:

High blood sugar- Eating more than you planned, exercising less than usual, eating too many carbohydrates, and stress.

Low blood sugar- Diabetes medicine, including taking the wrong amount or taking it at the wrong time, skipping a meal or waiting too long between meals, or drinking alcohol.

Treatment

Your doctor may suggest medication if your pancreas can still make some insulin. In general, diabetes medication can work by helping your pancreas make more insulin, helping insulin in your body work better, decreasing the amount of sugar your liver makes, blocking the breakdown of starches so they can't be turned into sugar, preventing the breakdown of hormones that help lower blood sugar, and preventing your kidneys from reabsorbing sugar.

Insulin- You will need insulin if your pancreas can't make enough. If you have to inject it with a syringe and needle, pen, or pump.

Intermittent Fasting- Intermittent fasting is any of various meal timing schedules that cycle between voluntary fasting and non-fasting over a given period. Methods of intermittent fasting include periodic fasting and daily time-restricted eating. Here are some changes that occur in your body when you fast:

The level of Human growth hormone (HGH) skyrocket, increasing as much as fivefold. This has benefits for fat loss and muscle gain, to name a few.

Insulin - Insulin sensitivity improves, and the level of insulin drops significantly. Lower insulin levels make stored body fat more accessible, leading to improved weight loss.

Cellular repair- When fasted, your cells initiate cellular repair processes.

Gene expression- There are changes in the function of genes related to longevity and protection against disease.

Some things that may help improve insulin sensitivity include:

1. Exercise- Physical activity helps build muscle that absorbs blood glucose and makes the body more sensitive to insulin.
2. Sleep- Getting enough sleep may help improve insulin sensitivity.
3. Reduce stress- Ongoing stress keeps your stress hormone levels high, stimulating nutrient breakdown and increasing blood sugar. A high level of stress hormones also reduces insulin sensitivity.
4. Lose a few pounds- Excess weight, especially belly fat, reduces insulin sensitivity and increases the risk of type-2 diabetes. Losing belly weight increases insulin sensitivity and reduces the risk of developing type-2 diabetes if you are pre-diabetic.
5. Diet- Eating a nutritious diet that is high in unsaturated fats and soluble fiber may help. Adding colorful vegetables and fruits also increases insulin sensitivity. Fruits that are good for diabetes include avocado- few carbohydrates, high fiber, and healthy fat.

People with diabetes can enjoy an avocado in moderation. Other fruits good for diabetes include plums, blueberries, strawberries, apples, and papaya.

Intermittent fasting also lowers cholesterol, clears skin, reduces blood sugar level, lowers triglycerides, reduces inflammation, and improves immunity. Fasting also allows your body to flush out damaged, unused cells and regenerate new, healthy cells. A balanced, healthy diet, along with intermittent fasting, results in overall optimum physical health.

Here are some steps you can take to lower your blood sugar:

- Eat a healthy diet- Eat plenty of fruits, vegetables, lean protein, whole grains, and legumes. Limit foods high in calories, saturated fat, sugar, and salt.
- Exercise regularly- Regular physical activity can help your body use sugar for energy and improve insulin sensitivity. Aim for 30 minutes of physical activity most days of the week.
- Manage your carb intake- Carbs are converted into sugar by the body, so it is important to monitor how many you eat. Choose nutrient-dense, high fiber, complex carbs over simple carbs.
- Stay hydrated- Drinking water helps your kidneys filter out excess sugar. Hot liquids can help you feel full and reduce snacking.
- Get enough sleep- Poor sleep can increase appetite and promote weight gain.
- Manage stress- Stress can affect blood sugar levels.
- Monitor your blood sugar levels- Check your blood sugar at least once a day, before and after meals and exercise.
- Eat more fiber- Fiber slows down the digestion of carbohydrates and sugar absorption.

Exercise

Regular Physical activity is one of the most important things you can do for your health. Being physically active can improve your mind, help manage weight, reduce the risk of disease, strengthen bones and muscles, and improve your ability to perform everyday activities. Exercise is good for optimizing health. Exercise is a physical activity that follows a planned format. It is done with repeated movements, with the goal of improving or keeping up one or more specific areas of physical fitness. There are four basic types of exercises that are important for adults to gain health benefits.

Endurance exercises- Endurance exercises are activities that increase your breathing and heart rate. They improve the health of your lungs and circulatory system. Having more endurance not only helps you stay healthier, but it can also improve your stamina for the tasks you need to do to live and do things on your own. Endurance exercises also may delay or prevent many diseases associated with aging, such as diabetes, colon cancer, heart disease, stroke, and others, and have been shown to reduce the overall deaths and hospitalization rates.

To build up stamina, you can do specific exercises, like walking, jogging, or any other activity that raises your heart rate and breathing for an extended period of time.

Do at least 30 minutes of endurance activities on most or all days of the week.

If you prefer, divide 30 minutes into short sessions of no less than 10 minutes each. The more vigorous the exercise, the greater the benefit.

Warm up and cool down with a light activity such as easy walking. Activities shouldn't make you breathe so hard that you can't talk. They shouldn't cause dizziness or chest pain.

When you are ready to progress, first increase the amount of time, then the difficulty of your activity.

Stretch after endurance exercises.

Strength exercises – strength exercises build up muscles, but they do more than just make you stronger. They may improve your independence by giving you more strength to do things on your own. Strength exercises also increase your metabolism, helping to keep your weight and blood sugar in check. Strength exercises may also help prevent osteoporosis.

Do strength exercises for all your major muscle groups at least twice a week, but not for the same muscle group on any two days in a row.

Gradually increase the amount of weight you use. It is the most important part of strength exercise. Start with a low amount of weight and increase it gradually.

When you are ready to progress, first increase the number of times you do the exercise, then increase the weight at a later session.

Do exercise 8 to 15 times; rest for a minute, and repeat it 8 to 15 more times.

Take 3 seconds to lift and 3 seconds to lower weight. If you can't lift a weight more than 8 times, it is too heavy; and if you can lift it more than 15 times, it is too light.

Avoid holding your breath while straining.

Stretch after strength exercises.

Balance Exercises- Balance exercises help prevent a common problems to older adults: falls, in older people. Falling is a major cause of broken hips and other injuries. Recent incidents of falls and injuries of older prominent Americans have brought attention to balance exercises to prevent and reduce the incidence of falls. Falling is a major cause of hip and other injuries that often lead to disability and loss of independence. Balance exercises build up your leg muscles.

One way to balance exercise is to balance on one foot, then the other. Tree pose in yoga is where you shift your weight onto your left leg, bend your right knee, and place your right foot on the inside of your left leg, either above or below your knee joint. Repeat with the other foot. This is a good exercise for balance.

Flexibility exercises- Flexibility exercises are stretching exercises. They are thought to help keep your body limber by stretching your muscles and the tissue that holds your body's structure in place.

Do stretching exercises after endurance and strength exercises, when your muscles are warm.

Do stretching exercises 3 to 5 times at each session.

Hold the stretched portion for 10 to 30 seconds.

Move slowly into position; never jerk into position.

Stretching may cause mild discomfort, but should not cause pain.

One of the popular stretch exercises is the calf stretch. Stand facing the wall 2 feet away. While standing, place your hands on a wall, with arms outstretched, elbows straight. Keeping your left knee slightly bent, toes of right foot slightly turned inwards, move your right foot back one or two feet, with your right heel and foot flat on the floor. You should feel a stretch on your right calf muscle. Keep your right knee straight and hold that position for 10 to 15 seconds. Repeat 3 to 5 times on each side.

Here is a description of ten exercises to tone every inch of your body.

- Lunges- Challenging your balance is an essential part of a well-rounded exercise routine. Lunges promote functional movements while also increasing strength in your legs and glutes.

  Start by standing with your feet, shoulders, and arms down at your sides.

  - Take a step forward with your right leg and bend your right knee as you do so, stopping when your thigh is parallel to the ground. Ensure that your right knee doesn't extend past your right foot.
  - Push up off your right foot and return to the starting position. Repeat with your left leg. This is one rep.
  - Complete three sets of 10 reps.
- Pushups- Pushups are one of the most basic yet effective bodyweight moves you can perform because of the number of muscles that are involved in performing them.
- Start in a plank position. Your core shoulder should be tight, your shoulders pulled down and back, and your neck neutral.
- Bend your elbows and begin to lower your body down to the floor. When your chest grazes it, extend your elbows and return to the start. Focus on keeping your elbows close to your body during the movement.

- Complete three sets of as many reps as possible. If you can't quite perform a standard pushup with good form, drop down to a modified stance on your knees-you will still reap many of the benefits from this exercise while building strength.
- Squats- Squats increase lower body and core strength, as well as flexibility in your lower back and hips, because they engage some of the largest muscles in the body. They also pack a major punch in terms of calories burned.
  - Start by standing straight, with your feet slightly wider than shoulder-width apart, and your arms at your sides
  - Brace your core and, keeping your chest and chin up, push your hips back and bend your knees as if you are going to sit in a chair.
  - Ensure your knees don't bow inward or outward, drop down until your thighs are parallel to the ground, and bring your arm out in front of you, and be in a comfortable position. Pause for a second, then extend your legs and return to the starting position.
  - Complete three sets of 20reps.
  - Standing overhead dumbbell press- Compound exercises, which utilize multiple joints and muscles, are perfect for an active person as they work several parts of your body at once. A standing overhead press is not only one of the best exercises you can do for your shoulders, but it also engages your upper back and core.
    Equipment: 10-pound dumbbells.
- Pick a light set of dumbbell-10 pounds to start- and start by standing. Either with your feet, shoulders width apart, or staggered. Move the weight overhead so your upper arms are parallel to the floor.
- Brace your core, begin to push up until your arms are fully extended above your head. Keep your head and neck stationary.
- After a brief pause, bend your elbows and lower the weight back down until your triceps muscle is parallel to the floor again.
- Complete three sets of 12 reps.

- Dumbbell rows- Dumbbell rows are also another compound exercise that strengthens multiple muscles in your upper body. Choose a moderate-weight dumbbell and ensure that you are squeezing at the top of the movement.

Equipment: 10-pound dumbbells

  - Start with a dumbbell in each hand.
  - Bend forward at the waist, so that your back is at a 45-degree angle to the ground. Be certain not to arch your back. Let your arms hang straight down. Ensure your neck is in line with your back and your core is engaged.
  - Starting with your right arm, bend your elbow and pull00 the weight straight up towards your chest, making sure to engage your lat and stopping just below your chest.
  - Return to the standing position and repeat with the left arm. This is one rep. Repeat 10 times for a 3-set.

Single-leg deadlifts- This is a balance exercise. Single-leg deadlifts require stability and leg strength. Grab a light to moderate dumbbell to complete this move.

Equipment: dumbbell

  - Begin standing with a dumbbell in your right hand and your knees slightly bent.
  - Hinging at the hips. Begin to kick your left leg straight back behind you, lowering the dumbbell down towards the ground.
  - When you reach a comfortable height with your left leg, slowly return to the starting position in a controlled motion, squeezing your right glute. Ensure that your pelvis stays square to the ground during the movement.
  - Repeat 10 to 12 reps before moving the weight to your left hand and repeating the same steps on the left leg. It's suggested to do three sets of 10-12 reps per side.

Burpees- Burpees are a super effective, whole body move that provides great bang for your cardiovascular endurance and muscle strength.

  - Start by standing upright with your feet shoulder-width apart and your arms down at your sides.

- With your hands out in front of you, start to squat down. When your hands reach the ground, pop your legs straight back into a pushup position.
- Jump your feet up to your palms by hinging at the waist. Get your feet as close to your hands as you can get, landing them outside your hands if necessary.
- Stand up straight, bringing your arms above your head, and jump.
- This is one rep. Continue three sets of 10 reps as a beginner.

Side planks- A healthy body requires a strong core at its foundation, so don't neglect core-specific moves like the side plank. Focus on the mind muscle connection and controlled movements to ensure you're completing this move effectively.

- Lie on your side with your left leg and foot stacked on top of your right leg and foot. Prop your upper body up by placing your right forearm on the ground and your elbow directly under your shoulder.
- Contract your core to stiffen your spine and lift your hips and knees off the ground, forming a straight line with your body.
- Return to the start in a controlled manner. Repeat three sets of 10-15 reps on one side, then switch.

Planks- Planks are an effective way to target both your abdominal muscles and your whole body. Planking stabilizes your core without straining your back the way sit-ups or crunches might.

- Begin a pushup position with your hand and toes firmly planted on the ground, your back straight, and your core tight.
- Keep your chin slightly tucked and your gaze just in front of your hands.
- Take a deep, controlled breaths while maintaining tension throughout your entire body, so your abs, shoulders, triceps, glutes, and quads re all engaged.
- Complete 2-3 sets of 30-second holds to start.
- Glute bridge- The glute bridge effectively works your entire posterior chain, which isn't only good for you, but it'll make your booty perkier, too.
  - Start by lying on the floor with your knees bent, feet flat on the ground, and arms straight at your sides with your palms facing down.

- Pushing through your heels, raising your hips off the ground by squeezing your core, glutes, and hamstrings. Your upper back and shoulders should still be in contact with the ground, and your core, down to your knees, should form a straight line.
- Pause 1-3 seconds at the top and return to the starting position.
- Complete 10-12 reps for three sets.

These fundamental exercises will do your body good.

Benefits of Physical Activity

Regular physical activity is one of the most important things you can do for your health. Being physically active can improve your brain health, help manage weight, reduce the risk of disease, strengthen bones and muscles, and improve your ability to do everyday activities. Immediate benefits of physical activities include:

Weight management- Both eating patterns and physical activity routines play a crucial role in weight management. To maintain your weight, work your way up to 150 minutes a week of moderate physical activity. You can achieve the goal of 150 minutes a week with 30 minutes a day, 5 days a week.

Cardiovascular disease- Heart disease and stroke are the leading causes of death in the United States. Getting at least 150 minutes a week of moderate physical activity can put you at a lower risk for these diseases. Regular physical activity can also lower your blood pressure and improve your cholesterol levels.

Type 2 Diabetes and Metabolic Syndrome- Regular physical activity can reduce your risk of developing type 2 diabetes and metabolic syndrome. Metabolic syndrome is a combination of too much fat around the waist, high blood pressure, low high-density lipoprotein (HDL) cholesterol, high triglycerides, and high blood sugar.

Infectious diseases- Physical activity lowers your risk for developing several kinds of cancers. Adults who participate in greater amounts of physical activity have reduced risk of developing cancers of the bladder, breast, colon, endometrium, esophagus, kidney, lung, and stomach.

Strengthening your bones and muscles- Muscles- Strengthening activities like lifting weights can help you increase or maintain your muscle mass and strength; This is important for older adults who experience reduced muscle mass and muscle strength with aging.

Improve daily activities and prevent falls- For older adults, doing a variety of physical activities improves physical function and decreases the risk of falls or injury from a fall.

Increase your chances of living longer- An estimated 110,000 deaths per year could be prevented if U.S. adults ages 40 and over increased their moderate-to vigorous physical activity by a small amount. Even 10 minutes more a day would make a difference.

Manage chronic health conditions & disabilities- Regular physical activity can reduce pain and improve function, mood, and quality of life for adults with arthritis. Help control blood sugar levels and lower the risk of heart disease and nerve damage for people with type 2 diabetes. Help support daily living activities and independence for people with disabilities.

Manage stress- Exercise helps reduce the levels of stress hormones such as cortisol in the body. It also increases positive hormones like endorphins and oxytocin (also known as the love hormones). These hormones not only help you feel good, but they also help you fall asleep faster and stay asleep longer.

Walking- Walking is a low-impact exercise, easy on your joints, and can be done just about anywhere. There are specific benefits after eating. A stroll around the block after a meal can be a healthy burst. Just a few minutes of walking after eating can lower your blood pressure. Studies have shown that for adults with high blood pressure, walking is effective in reducing systolic and diastolic blood pressure. Those with more severe hypertension saw a more significant reduction. Walking after eating can aid in digestion. Walking stimulates the stomach and intestines. This can help food move through the digestive system more rapidly. Walking after eating may help regulate your blood sugar. It is also best to start walking as soon as possible after finishing a meal. Since blood sugar levels tend to spike between 60 and 90 minutes after eating, walking can boost your metabolism, helping you burn more calories from fat. On average, a person who weighs 150 pounds will burn about 199 calories per mile walking at a mild pace. The average person takes about 20 minutes to walk a mile, so a 30-minute walk after a meal at a mild pace could burn 150 calories, if not more. Walking after a meal can improve your mood. Somehow, you can include walking in your daily routine by parking your car farther away from the entrance of your office. Taking stairs instead of the elevator. Make a habit of walking after meal time and creating within your routine whenever possible.

Yoga for the Improvement of Overall Health

Yoga is more than just another form of fitness. The discipline transcends the physicality of the postures. Yoga is also a mental and spiritual practice, in the sense that the work that goes into aligning your body can also be used to align your mind. The word yoga means to "yoke" or union, and the discipline aims to bring the mind and the body into sync with each other. This is accomplished through the three main components of yoga: posture, breathing, and meditation. It is through the physical practice of doing yoga poses and breathing that the individual is enabled to then sit and meditate, allowing the mind and the body to become one.

The Eight Limbs of Yoga

One of the most famous yogic texts is the Yoga Sutras. The classic book, compiled by second-century B.C. scholar Patanjali, stated the guidelines for yoga practice, including the eight-limbed path a yoga student should follow. According to Patanjali, the eight limbs of yoga are:

- Yamas (abstinence)
- Niyamas (observance)
- Asana (posture)
- Pranayama (breath control)
- Pratyahara (sense withdrawal)
- Dharna (concentration)
- Dhayana (meditation)
- Samadhi (contemplation, absorption, or super-conscious state)

The first two limbs of yoga, yamas and niyamas, are concerned with spiritual aspects of life and will be discussed in the spirituality section. The third and fourth limbs of yoga asanas and pranayama will be covered in this section on physical health. Fifth. Sixth, the seventh and eighth limbs of yoga, pratyahara, dharna, dhyana, and samadhi, are linked with the mind and will be covered under the mental/ emotional section.

Asanas

Yoga exercises focus on the health of the spine, its strength, and flexibility. The spinal column houses the nervous system by maintaining spinal flexibility and strength through yoga exercise. Circulation is increased and the nerves are ensured their supply of nutrients and oxygen. The asanas also affect the internal organs and the endocrine system.

The practice of yoga improves one's sense of balance, posture, strength, and general body comfort. The practice of yoga can improve mental and emotional health. Yoga improves a person's ability to sleep better and boosts energy levels. The awareness of breath and body, which is an integral part of yoga practice, can enable practitioner to become attuned to their own physiological response to stress, and to begin counteracting those stress responses. Studies show that people's concentration and attention spans improve as a result of yoga, and even memory can gain a boost. Yoga instills a sense of calm and relaxation, and it boosts stamina as well. Thus, postures in yoga are made to strengthen your body from the inside to the outside.

Pranayama, or the science of yoga breathing, is the fourth limb of the discipline of yoga. In Sanskrit, prana means "life force energy", and ayama means to "control or extend". Together they form the word pranayama, which means "extension of life force" or breath control. The practice of yoga calls for us to pay close attention to the practice of breathing in and out that one usually takes for granted.

The complete yoga breath

The complete yoga breath forms an integral part of relaxation. This not only increases the intake of oxygen as you inhale and eliminates toxins such as carbon dioxide as you exhale, but also massages and tones the internal organs as your diaphragm moves up and down with each breath. Focusing on your breathing calms your thoughts and makes your mind steady, while the brain improves your concentration.

Yoga breathing exercises (deep breathing)

- Sit cross-legged with your spine as erect as possible. Extend up through your spine to lengthen the back of your neck and lift your head. Open your chest and relax your shoulders. Place your hand on your abdomen, below the navel. Breathe deeply so that your hands rise and fall slowly in time with your breath. Continue 10 breaths.

- Place your hands on your rib cage and breathe slowly and deeply. As you inhale, your ribcage expands and your diaphragm moves down to massage your abdominal organs. As you exhale, your rib cage deflates and your diaphragm moves up to give your heart a gentle massage. Continue for 10 breaths.

- Place your hands just beneath your collarbones. Relax your arms and drop your elbows towards the floor. Breathe deeply and slowly into the top of your chest. This technique increases awareness of the breath, expands and deepens the thorax, and encourages your lungs to take in oxygen to their full capacity. Continue 10 breaths.

Alternate Nostril Breathing

Alternate nostril breathing is another variation of pranayama breathing practices. This exercise involves pinching one nostril at a time to help you control the pace and pattern of breathing.

- Blocking the right nostril with your right thumb, slowly breathe in through your left nostril for 6 seconds.
- Block your left nostril with your index finger while holding your breath for 6 seconds.
- Unblock your right nostril and breathe out through your right nostril for 6 seconds.
- Breath in with your right nostril for 6 seconds.
- Block your right nostril with your thumb and hold for 6 seconds.
- Unlock your left nostril and breathe out through your left nostril for 6 seconds.
- Repeat for several rounds of breathing.
  - Health Benefits of yoga include:
  - Regulate blood pressure and heart rate
  - Reducing pain and inflammation
  - Increase energy
  - Improving joint health
  - Relieving stress, anxiety, and depression.
  - Boosting immune function
  - Relieving digestive issues

o   Improving sleep

o   Increasing strength, balance, and flexibility

o   Supporting weight management.

Sleep

Like eating nutritious food and exercising, getting quality sleep is an important component of overall health. Sleep is a normal physiological function, designed by nature to refresh and reboot the body and mind. Good sleep is essential for sound health and well-being. Quality sleep is associated with a balanced life. Most adults should get between seven and nine hours of sleep each night. While sleeping, the body performs a number of repairing and maintaining processes that affect nearly every part of the body. As a result, good night's sleep, or a lack of sleep, can impact the body both mentally and physically. During sleep, the body rests, cleans, and purifies itself, rebuilds, grows, and heals itself. Sleep experts agree that there are numerous benefits to consistently getting a full night's rest. Health benefits of sleep include improved mood, a healthy heart, regulation of blood sugar, improved mental function, restoring the immune system, stress relief, and maintaining a healthy weight.

How sleep works

As you sleep, your brain works to physically repair your body. Your brain cycle goes through four stages of sleep multiple times a night. The first three stages are considered non-rapid eye movement (NREM) sleep, and the fourth cycle is REM sleep. Each stage of the cycle is assigned a certain brain wave pattern and physical activities.

Sleep cycle

Stage 1- This non-REM lasts just one to seven minutes, as you transition from being awake to falling asleep. Your heart rate, eye movement, and brain waves slow down, and your muscles relax.

Stage 2- This stage lasts 10 to 25 minutes over the course of a night. During this stage of light sleep, you experience a lower body temperature and more relaxed muscles. Your heart and breath slow even more.

Stage 3- This stage lasts 20 to 40 minutes. This stage is known as deep sleep. In this stage, your heart and breath reach their slowest rates. Your brain waves slow further, and it is difficult to wake you up. In the first half of the night, this stage is longer. In the later cycles, it becomes shorter. The brain activity during this period is an identification pattern of what are known as delta waves. Experts believe that this stage is critical to restorative sleep, bodily recovery, and growth. It may also boost the immune system, contribute to insight thinking, creativity, and memory functions.

Stage4- This stage is REM sleep. About 90 minutes after you fall asleep, REM sleep begins. During REM, your breathing and heart rate speed up. Your eyes move rapidly, hence the name of this stage. A majority of dreams occur during REM sleep. Your brain temporarily paralyzes your muscles, so you do not act out those dreams and hurt yourself. While the first REM stage may last only a few minutes, the late stages can last for around an hour. Total REM stages make up 25% of sleep, in adults. In a typical night, a person goes through four to six sleep cycles.

Sleep Problems

It is estimated that 50 percent of the general population and 70 percent of older persons have a sleeping problem. Sleep problems include insomnia and sleep apnea. Insomnia is associated with stress and anxiety, a poor sleep environment, and lifestyle. Your physical, emotional, and mental health all improve with better sleep. To get better night sleep, practice sleep hygiene. Sleep hygiene refers to a set of recommendations, habits, and behaviors designed to promote quality sleep. Educating a person on sleep hygiene is often part of treating insomnia. Sleep hygiene includes:

Follow regular sleep schedule- Go to bed and wake up at the same time every day.

Carefully choose food and dinner - A sleep-friendly diet includes a variety of foods, with adequate protein and fiber. It also helps to avoid eating anything spicy or fatty close to bedtime to prevent heartburn and reflux from interfering with your sleep. You may also want to consider lowering your caffeine and alcohol consumption, too. Both disrupt sleep, especially when ingested in the evening.

Get some sun and exercise- Reinforce your circadian rhythms with plenty of exposure to natural light, especially early in the day. For an extra energy boost, pair your sunlight time with exercise. Daily exercise has been shown to improve sleep.

Make your bedroom pleasant- A calm bedroom environment can make it easier to relax. Keep the bedroom cool, dark, and as quiet as possible to promote sound sleep. It is also important to invest in a mattress, pillow, and bedding set that makes you feel comfortable. The ideal bedroom temperature for sleep falls between 66- and 70-degrees Fahrenheit. Incorporating these practices into your routine may help improve your sleep.

Sleep Apnea: Obstructive sleep apnea (OSA) is a disorder in which a person's breathing is obstructed frequently during sleep. Sleep apnea treatment includes lifestyle changes, such as weight loss and the use of breathing assistance devices at night, such as a continuous positive airway pressure (CPAP) machine. Sleeping on your side with your back straight also helps. Other methods, such as using a humidifier, avoiding sedatives, reducing nasal congestion, and exercising, may also help.

Behaviors for a longer, healthier life

Key measures for improving your total health include prevention of heart disease, strokes, cancer, disability, and hypertension, the major causes of death and disabilities in our society. According to the World Health Organization, 80 percent of heart disease, stroke, and type 2 diabetes, and 40 percent of cancer could be prevented, with improvements to diet and lifestyle.

- Diet: A healthy diet is a calorie-controlled, plant-based diet with less meat, sugar, and salt and more protein. This means eating a lot of vegetables, fruits, and nuts, choosing whole-grain foods, limiting processed foods, and restricting or even avoiding red meat altogether. Keep your body well hydrated all the time. Clean water is the best drink.
- Regular physical activity: Physical activity keeps your heart and circulation system healthy and provides protection against numerous chronic diseases. It can also strengthen muscles, which can reduce older people's risk of falls. If we spend adult years building up our muscle mass, our strength, our balance, our cardiovascular endurance, then as the body ages, we are starting from a stronger place. The best exercise is any activity you enjoy doing and will stick with. The American Heart Association recommends 150 minutes of moderate-intensity exercise per week. Walking for a little more than 20 minutes a day is beneficial.
- Healthy sleep: You should get 7-9 hours of continuous sleep. So, it is important to maintain proper sleep hygiene, such as going to bed and waking up about the same time every day. Avoid napping in the afternoon for longer than 30 minutes. And expose

yourself to regular sunlight during the daytime. Consistently good sleep can add several years to a person's life. Sleep is also important for brain health. As people get older, they need more sleep.

- Maintain a healthy weight: As measured in body mass index (BMI), the idea is to maintain your BMI in the 20-25 range. Obesity has become a major problem in the U.S. and is a major cause of hypertension, diabetes, and cancer. Mindful eating with exercise is the right thing to do.

- Maintain ideal blood pressure (B.P.); Hypertension is a common problem and can lead to many complications like heart disease, strokes, and kidney disease, just to name a few. Guidelines suggest a reading of less than 120/80 in mmHg as normal for most people.

- Control your blood sugar: Diabetes Mellitus (DM), especially Type 2, causes heart disease and chronic kidney disease. HbA1C is the best parameter to decide if your DM is well controlled. Normal is 5.6 or below. A level of 5.7 to 6.4 indicates pre-diabetes, and anything over 6.4 means you have diabetes. So, try to keep your HbA1C as close to 6.5 or below when possible.

- Control your bad cholesterol (LDL-c); Heart disease from coronary atherosclerosis is still the number 1 killer. The main substrate of the atherosclerosis plaque is LDL cholesterol. So, keep your LDL as low as possible. It should be less than 100. A low-fat diet coupled with appropriate drug therapy, especially statins, is the way to go.

- Don't smoke or drink too much: Tobacco products have become the largest, single preventable cause of death in America. In spite of the warnings by the Surgeon General, people still smoke in general. A smoker dies 20 years earlier than a non-smoker. Excessive drinking raises the risk of heart disease and atrial fibrillation, liver disease, and several types of cancer. More than one drink per day for women and two for men is harmful to health.

Nearly half of the American adults have high blood pressure, 40% have high cholesterol, and more than one-third have pre-diabetes. All the healthy behaviors mentioned above will help manage these conditions and prevent them from developing into even more serious diseases. It is also critical to follow your doctor's advice to keep things under control,

Section 3:
Mental/Emotional Health
Mental/Emotional Health Issues

Physical health and mental health are intertwined. Your brain is a part of your body, and your body communicates with your brain to help you function. When your heart is at peace, the mind is at ease. The brain refers to the physical organ in our head that supports the functioning of the mind. Mind is the element of a person that enables them to be aware of the world and their experiences, to think, and feel the faculty of consciousness and thoughts. Mind is the activity of thinking, using logic and/ or reason to arrive at insight and conclusions about people, events, belief systems, and life. The brain is the physical organ inside the skull of humans, while the mind is the sense of consciousness that takes place inside the mind. The forebrain is a mammal's largest and most advanced part in humans. The outer layer of the forebrain is called the cerebral cortex, in which high-level processes such as thinking, planning, language processing, decision-making, and coordination of motor information take place. Intellectual functioning covers a broad range of topics, including being open to new ideas, engaging in activities that sharpen your mind, learning new skills, and sharing thoughts and ideas with others. Intelligence stems from the cerebral cortex of the brain. Frontal and prefrontal lobes of the cerebral cortex are deeply involved in mental health functioning, such as cognition, judgment, and logical planning. On the other hand, subcortical functioning in the forebrain comes from the limbic system. The limbic system is associated with aspects of emotions, motivation and memory. The thalamus, hypothalamus, amygdala, hippocampus, and cingulate gyrus are significant parts of the limbic system and play a crucial role in our emotional experience.

Thalamus- The Thalamus is a part of the forebrain that functions as a sensory station in the brain. It relays information coming from our senses to the brain.

Hypothalamus- Hypothalamus lies below the thalamus. It is the size of an almond and accounts for less than 1% of the weight of the brain, weighing 4 grams out of 1400 grams of the brain. It performs a wide range of functions that are vital for our survival. It plays a role in maintaining homeostasis in the body. It is involved in sleep, body temperature, pleasure, sexual functioning, thirst, and hunger. The feeling of love does not come from the heart; it comes from the hypothalamus. The reason love is associated with the heart is that the sensation of love is felt at the heart, but love originates in the hypothalamus. Feelings associated with romantic love arise when the brain's hypothalamus orders the pituitary gland to release the hormone oxytocin, which contributes to physical intimacy, like cuddling and loving experiences.

Amygdala- Amygdala is a part of the limbic system that plays a role in our emotions of fear and aggression.

Hippocampus- The Hippocampus of the limbic system plays a role in short-term and long-term memory. Our strong emotions stir up when we remember past traumatic or ecstatic moments of our lives.

Cingulate gyrus- The Cingulate gyrus is involved with emotion formation and processing, learning, and memory. The combination of these three makes the cingulate gyrus highly influential in linking motivational outcomes to behavior.

When our limbic system (emotional brain) is aligned with our cerebral cortex (logical thinking brain), then we have harmony between emotional and mental health. It is important to recognize that emotional and mental health are interlinked. Emotional well-being can help people manage their mental disorders better, as well as provide an outlet for dealing with stress and other psychological issues. On the other hand, good emotional well-being can be disrupted if there is an underlying issue with our mental health.

Emotional health is about how we think and feel. It is about our sense of well-being, our ability to cope with life events as they occur in our lives. We acknowledge our emotions as well as those of others. Emotional health is your ability to cope with both positive and negative emotions, which includes your awareness of them. Emotional health has more to do with emotional awareness, emotional regulation, and coping skills. People make choices primarily dictated by either their heads (reason) or their hearts (feelings). The thinking functions help us see things logically; the feelings function helps us by caring. The basic emotions that drive us are fear, love, grief, greed, joy, and anger. Daniel Goleman, author of "Emotional Intelligence," asserts that IQ contributes about 20 percent to the factors that determine life success, which leaves 80 percent to other forces.

Emotional intelligence can be described as the ability to monitor and control one's emotions and behavior at work and in social settings. Two essential components of emotional intelligence are personal competence and social competence. Personal competence involves keeping disruptive emotions and impulses in check. Social competence refers to the competence that determines how we handle relationships, sensing other thoughts, feelings, and intentions; listening openly and sending convincing messages; and negotiating and resolving disagreements. Lack of emotional expressions or becoming extremely emotional causes emotional imbalance. Emotional imbalance also develops when we become fixated on a single emotion. Emotional health blends emotional intelligence and emotional regulation.

Signs that you are struggling with emotional problems.

You are feeling drained all the time.

Sleeping too much or too little

Neglecting personal hygiene.

Anxious or irritated with loved ones.

Physical signs of stress, like high blood pressure or heart palpitations.

Confidence or self-esteem is affected.

Five characteristics of an emotionally healthy person

1. They are self-aware and can perceive themselves accordingly and understand how their behavior comes across to others.
2. Emotional agility- Regulate cognitive ability, individual ability to deal with stresses and discomforts in work and daily living, ability to adapt, align, and perform well.
3. Have coping skills- Strong and healthy coping skills, practice meditation and relaxation, spend quality time with friends, and find time for hobbies.
4. Live with purpose.
5. Managing stress levels.

Taking active steps towards emotional and mental health can lead to the following:

Improve emotional regulation.

Better self-esteem and confidence.

Increased motivation and productivity.

A higher sense of overall well-being

Emotional and mental health topics include managing depression, anxiety, stress, and low self-esteem effectively. Mental health issues can range from mild cognitive impairment, such as loss of concentration, to problems such as schizophrenia and bipolar disorder.

Activities that help improve emotional /mental health include

Express feelings through art, writing, or music.

Talking about worries and concerns with friends and family,

Develop positive coping skills such as mindfulness, meditation, or exercise.

Practicing self-care, such as getting enough rest. Eating well. And engaging in activities like hobbies or sports.

Seeking support from a mental health professional if necessary.

Taking a holistic approach to overall well-being.

The bottom line is that emotional health and mental health should not be viewed as separate entities, but rather as interrelated components of overall wellness.

Mental Health

Mental health refers to your psychological, behavioral, and emotional well-being. It pertains to your ability to cope with the daily struggles of life. Many factors affect your mental health, including your genetics(nature), life experiences (nurture), and your perceptions and efforts. Even though the nature and nurture controversy continues, the third most significant part of your perceptions and efforts is sometimes overlooked in mental health research. Statistics indicate that one in five adults in the U.S. experiences mental illness each year, according to the National Alliance on Mental Illness. Mental health disorder is significantly affected by the way we think, feel, and behave. It may be caused by genetics, biochemistry, stress, trauma, or some combination of all these factors. Risk factors pertaining to mental health disorders include:

Genetics- Having a history of mental illness in the family increases the risk of developing a mental health disorder.

Chemistry- The balance of chemicals in the brain affects certain mental illnesses.

Stress- Unmanaged stress, particularly that which is chronic or cumulative, can lead to an increased risk for mental illness.

Trauma leads to the development of post-traumatic stress disorder (PTSD) and can increase the likelihood of developing a mental health disorder. Dysfunctional family upbringing and societal factors create circumstances that increase the likelihood of mental illness.

First thing to address mental health is to make a proper assessment. These include bio-psycho-social assessment (BPSA), presenting problem, and clinical interview, including mental status examination.

Mental Status Examination (MSE)

To determine the extent of mental health illness, a psychologist or psychotherapist conducts a bio-psycho-social assessment. This author, in his psychotherapy practice, conducted numerous such assessments, which include presenting mental health problems, onset of the problem, duration, frequency, and intensity of the problem, and how it is impacting the patient's mental health, social, occupational, and interpersonal relationships. Areas to look into are history and current situation of the family, birth, childhood, and adolescent development, educational background, work experience, financial situation, history of physical /sexual abuse, psycho social development, including marital and family history, medical concerns, substance abuse history, and mental status examination.

The mental status examination (MSE) is a crucial component of clinical assessment in psychotherapy practice. It is a structured way of observing and describing a patient's appearance, attitude, behavior, mood, affect, speech, thought process, thought content, perception, cognition, insight, and judgment.

The purpose of MSE is to obtain a comprehensive cross-sectional description of the patient's mental state, which, when combined with the bio-psycho-social assessment, allows the clinician to make an accurate diagnosis and formulation, which are required for coherent treatment planning. Significant distress and impairment in interpersonal, social, occupational, or other important areas of functioning are noted at this time. Psychological tests are at times utilized to supplement the clinical interview to diagnose a particular mental illness per "Diagnostic and Statistical Manual of Mental Disorders", Fifth Edition (DSM-5).

Mental Health Disorders

An estimated one in five U.S. adults lives with a mental illness (57.8 million). Nearly 1 in 25 (10 million) adults in U.S. live with a serious mental illness. One-half of all chronic mental illness begins by the age of 14, three-quarters by the age of 24. Mental illness includes many different conditions that vary in degrees of severity, ranging from mild to moderate to severe. Major mental disorders in adults include anxiety disorders, mood disorders, psychotic disorders, substance use and addictive disorders.

Anxiety Disorders

The most common category of mental health disorder is anxiety disorder, impacting 40 million adults aged 18 and older. Anxiety disorder causes people to experience distressing and frequent fear and apprehension. Five major anxiety and anxiety-related disorders include generalized anxiety disorder (GAD), panic disorder, phobic disorder, obsessive-compulsive disorder (OCD), and post-traumatic stress disorder (PTSD).

Generalized Anxiety Disorder (GAD)- The most common anxiety disorder is generalized anxiety disorder. It is characterized by excessive worry and issues and situations that an individual experiences almost every day. And that worry is out of proportion to the reality of the situation. Excessive anxiety and worry occurring for at least six months. Further, the individual finds it difficult to control the worry. The anxiety and worry are usually accompanied by restlessness, fatigue, difficulties in concentration, irritability, muscle tension, and disturbed sleep. Further, the anxiety, worry, or physical symptoms cause clinically significant distress or impairment in social, occupational, or other important areas of functioning.

Panic Disorder- The essential feature of panic disorder is the presence of recurrent, unexpected panic attacks followed by at least one month of persistent concern about having another panic attack, worry about the possibility of additional panic attacks, and or significant maladaptive change in behavior related to the attack.

Phobic Disorder- Anxiety disorders characterized by intense fear of a specific object or situation. Phobic disorders include agoraphobia, specific phobia, and social phobia. Agoraphobia is an excessive fear of being in places from which escape might be difficult or where help might not be available if one were to experience panic. People affected with agoraphobia avoid any place- the mall, the grocery store, or the movie theatre. Specific phobia involves a persistent fear and avoidance of a specific object or situation, such as an animal, height, bridge, or other specific stimuli. They are one of the most common disorders worldwide, affecting 9% of American adults. Social phobia includes an irrational, persistent fear of being negatively evaluated by others in a social situation. A person with a social phobia (also known as social anxiety) may have extreme fear of embarrassment or humiliation in a social setting. It is estimated that 12% of American adults will experience a social phobia at sometimes in their lives.

Obsessive-compulsive disorder (OCD) is a condition characterized by recurrent thoughts or images that intrude on a person's consciousness or awareness. Compulsions are repetitive behaviors that a person feels a strong urge to perform. OCD is an anxiety disorder in which a person experiences recurrent obsessions or compulsions that he or she feels cannot be controlled. Recurrent obsessions cause great personal distress.

Post-Traumatic Stress Disorder (PTSD) requires that the person repeatedly experience the ordeal in the form of distressing memories, nightmares, frightening thoughts, or flashbacks episodes. Approximately 3.5 % of U.S. adults are diagnosed with PTSD in a given year. More than twice as many females as males experience the following exposure to a trauma, typically sexual assault. Soldiers are at high risk for developing PTSD as military conflict is a source of trauma. About 19% of Vietnam veterans developed PTSD at some point after the war. Twenty percent of the recovery workers and volunteers at the World Trade Center experienced symptoms of PTSD. More than 19% of people experienced PTSD after Hurricane Katrina.

Causes of Anxiety

Biological, psychological, and socio-cultural factors contribute to anxiety. The functioning of several neurotransmitters has been linked to anxiety disorders. Abnormal activity of norepinephrine, serotonin, or gamma-aminobutyric acid (GABA) may be involved in panic attacks. Abnormal activity of GABA has been linked to people with GAD, while problems in serotonin regulation have been suggested as a cause for OCD and PTSD.

Anxiety disorders tend to run in families, suggesting a genetic link. Neuroimaging research on individuals with GAD shows difficulty in regulating an area of the brain that lessens the activity of the amygdala (part of the limbic system or emotional brain). As a result, the amygdala becomes overactive, and the person experiences a high level of anxiety and difficulties in regulating emotions. Similarly, neuroimaging studies on people with PTSD suggest dysfunction in the amygdala that may contribute to their emotional and memory-related symptoms.

Psychological factors also help in explaining anxiety. The psychoanalytical perspective suggests that anxiety is linked to unresolved unconscious conflicts. The social learning perspective suggests that phobias are learned. When a neutral stimulus is paired with a stimulus that naturally elicits fear. Cognitive research suggests that our thinking processes play a role in developing an anxiety disorder. In particular, people who perceive situations and objects as uncontrollable, unpredictable, dangerous, and disgusting are more vulnerable to anxiety disorders. People with anxiety disorders also tend to process negative information rather than positive or neutral information about an event. Humanistic psychologists attribute anxiety to an unrealistic self-image. An unrealistic self-image results in being overly critical of oneself.

Social and cultural factors are involved in anxiety. Women are more likely than men to be diagnosed with an anxiety disorder. This gender difference has been attributed to several factors: women's relative lack of power in society, difficulties in gender role socialization, making it acceptable for women to report fear, and a greater likelihood that women will be victims of violence, crime, or abuse.

Treatment

For generalized anxiety disorder (GAD), both drug and psychological treatment are quite effective. Benzodiazepines are most often prescribed for GAD. Commonly prescribed benzodiazepine drugs are Valium. Xanax, Klonopin, and Ativan. Benzodiazepines can cause physical and psychological dependence, tolerance, and withdrawal symptoms, and there is a risk of being abused by susceptible individuals. That is why sometimes non-benzodiazepine selective serotonin reuptake inhibitors (SSRIs) are the first line of drug treatment. For GAD, SSRIs work by stopping nerve cells in the brain from reabsorbing serotonin, which is a chemical that plays a vital role in mood regulation. In the short term, psychological treatment seems to confer about the same benefit as drugs in the treatment of GAD, but the psychological treatments are probably more effective in the long run. During cognitive behavior therapy sessions, patients confront anxiety-provoking images and thoughts head-on. The patient learns to use cognitive behavior therapy and other coping techniques to counteract and control the worry process.

For panic disorder, SSRIs such as Prozac and Paxil are effective in the treatment of panic disorder. High-potency benzodiazepines such as Xanax work quickly, but are hard to stop because of psychological and physical dependence and addiction. Therefore, not recommended strongly as an SSRI. Psychological treatment focuses on the therapist's attempt to create a "mini" panic attack in the office, and the patient learn to face the feared situation and cope with the situation without having a panic attack.

For phobias, systematic desensitization experiences are quite effective, where a patient replaces a fear or anxiety response with an incompatible response of relaxation. The aim of systematic desensitization is to have a patient learn how to relax in the face of particular feared stimuli in a graded step-by-step process.

For PTSD, cognitive therapy is used to correct the negative assumptions about the trauma, such as blaming oneself in some way, feeling guilty, or both. Some of the drugs, such as Prozac and Paxil, are effective in the treatment of anxiety associated with PTSD.

For OCD, tricyclic antidepressants are found to be quite effective. Psychological treatment involves exposure and ritual prevention, whereby the rituals are actively prevented and the patient is gradually exposed to feared thoughts or situations.

Mood Disorders

Mood disorders affect one in 10 adults. A person suffering from mood disorders may feel sad, empty, with feelings of hopelessness, low self-esteem, excessive guilt, and decreased energy. The most common mood disorder is major depressive disorder. Sometimes referred to as clinical depression, it is characterized by low mood and loss of interest in daily life. This practitioner has observed that patients with mild depression benefited from psychotherapy, patients with moderate depression benefited from a combination of medication and psychotherapy, and patients with severe depression benefited from anti depression medication and inpatient treatment.

This therapist has developed a "Depression Management Program" in his clinical practice to help depressed patient overcome their depression and lead a depression free life. Most people muddle through their depression the best way they can. However, some people remain in a depressed mood and need help. The major techniques utilized in this program are cognitive behavior therapy (CBT). This form of therapy places emphasis on learning how to master your internal worlds of thoughts, feelings, and motivation. The basic principle of this approach is that how you think about experiences determines how you react emotionally.

Cause of Depression

Major depression stems from many bio-psychosocial factors, including genetic factors, stress hormones, and lack of neurotransmitters, specifically norepinephrine and serotonin. Psychological factors include learned helplessness and negative thinking. Social and cultural factors include adverse life experiences during childhood. Biological, psychological, and social factors that are unique to women may explain their vulnerability to depressive disorder.

Three major treatment modalities are: Biological intervention, including antidepressant medication. Cognitive behavior therapy and interpersonal therapy. Cognitive therapy is discussed under stress, anxiety, and anger management. Interpersonal therapy is elaborated in interpersonal relationships. Depression combined with anxiety contributes to a sense of hopelessness and helplessness and, at times, leads to suicidal thoughts and attempts. This practitioner developed a suicide prevention program and has provided training to other clinicians on how to observe obvious and subtle signs of suicide and take appropriate steps to intervene. Supportive counseling, cognitive therapy, and family support are crucial to build up hope in a person's life. Nearly one-third of the adult population in the U.S. in 2023 reported symptoms of anxiety and depression.

Suicide

According to new CDC data released from 2011 to 2021, nearly 3 in 5 (57%) of U.S. teen girls felt persistently sad or hopeless. In 2021, teen girls experienced twice the sadness as boys. More than 50,000 Americans died by suicide in 2023. Women are roughly three times more likely to attempt suicide than men; however, men are roughly three times more likely to take their own lives than women. The reason men die from suicide more is that men use violent methods like guns to take their lives, while women overdose on pills, get hospitalized, and most of them are saved. Most of the people with suicidal thoughts do not want to die; what they are generally seeking is relief or escape from an intolerable situation in which they are experiencing more stress, pain, grief, anguish, alienation, anger, frustration, disappointment, guilt, or illness than they can bear. Hopelessness, helplessness, and haplessness are three words that fit the description of the typical suicidal person. Hope is the light at the end of the tunnel. And as long as that light is visible, people will stay alive. One of the things in counseling the suicidal person is to build as strong a component of hope as possible. A concomitant of hopelessness is often helplessness. The typical suicidal person is very likely not only viewing his/her situation as hopeless, but also to see himself/herself as being absolutely helpless to take any meaningful action to alter his/her predicament. The third is haplessness. Suicidal person's family had incredibly sad lives. Family has a history of suicide, mental illness, chronic depression, desertion, alcohol/drug abuse, child abuse, spouse abuse, incest, or a dire financial situation.

Marilyn Monroe's life represents the typical example of haplessness as it relates to suicidality. Her father would never acknowledge paternity, nor speak with her. Her mother was chronically depressed and often institutionalized because of depression. She had an uncle who died in a mental institution. She has another uncle who died of alcoholism. She lived in a series of foster homes and was raped by one of her foster fathers. She had three marriages, which ended in divorce. She was having contractual problems with her studio shortly before her suicide. There is no simple cause of suicide, only causes.

About 75 % of suicidal people give warning signals. Clusters of warning signals are:

Sadness, frustration, disappointment, guilt, alienation, depression, loneliness, physical illness, anguish, or mental illness.

Some of the subtle warning signs are;

- Avoiding social situations for no particular reason.
- Indifference and, at times, sloppy performance at work or school.
- Alcohol or drug abuse.
- Giving up personal hygiene and positive habits.
- Careless about taking medications.
- Driving recklessly or engaging in risky behavior.

- Talking about feelings of shame, guilt, or hopelessness.
- Giving away possessions.

Some of the obvious signs are: wanting to die, great guilt or shame, being a burden to others, feeling empty, hopeless, having no reason to live, extremely sad, anxious and agitated.

To help a suicidal person

Establish trust and rapport with the person. This can be done by active listening, showing empathy, and conveying a genuine belief that the person has value and worth. The next step is to explain why the person is considering suicide. Avoid judging or shaming the person, but rather provide non-judgmental support. Talk about options and resources that may be available, and that person is not alone. At times, it may be necessary to hospitalize a suicidal person for constant monitoring. Provide psychiatric and psychological intervention as needed. Suicide crisis line call or text 988.

Bipolar Disorder

Bipolar disorder is characterized by mood swings from mania episodes to depressive episodes. Manic episodes may include symptoms such as high energy, reduced need for sleep, and loss of touch with reality. Depressive episodes may include symptoms such as low energy, low motivation, and loss of interest in daily activities. Symptoms of bipolar disorder are: feeling increasingly high or euphoric, delusions of self-importance, high levels of creativity, energy, and activity, experiencing loss of sleep or no sleep, poor appetite and weight loss, racing thoughts and speech, highly irritated, impatient, or aggressive. Treatment consists of psychotropic medication and psychotherapy.

Psychotic Disorder

Those suffering from psychotic disorders may be unable to understand what is real and what is not. An excess of dopamine is usually involved in this serious mental disorder. This disorder involves full-blown schizophrenia accompanied by delusions, hallucinations, or disordered thinking or behavior. Schizoaffective disorder causes patients to experience both psychotic symptoms and mood symptoms. During my private practice, I insisted that my patients be on psychiatric medication prescribed by a psychiatrist before enrolling in psychotherapy. Patients

66

with psychotic and bipolar disorders must be on psychotropic medication before psychotherapy sessions start. Only then, when the patient's chemical balance is controlled and behavior is stabilized to a great degree, can the patient focus on psychotherapy sessions, benefit, and become stable.

Substance Abuse and Addictive Disorders

Addiction is a condition of being dependent on a particular substance, thing, or activity. Drug addiction is defined as a chronic, relapsing disorder characterized by compulsive drug seeking and use despite adverse consequences. It involves functional changes to brain circuits involved in reward, stress, and self-control. It is a state of psychological or physical dependence (or both) on the use of a substance. Craving and urges for the substance are the main path of complex motivational forces determining the overt addictive behavior. Addiction to drug misuse involves alcohol, tobacco, cannabis, opiates, cocaine, and prescription drug abuse. About 38% of adults in 2017 battled an illicit drug use disorder. That same year, I was one of 8 adults who struggled with both alcohol and drug use simultaneously. In 2017, 8.5 million American adults suffered from both a mental health disorder and a substance abuse disorder or co-occurring disorder (also known as dual diagnosis disorder). 11.7% Americans 12 and older use illegal drugs. 53 million or 19.4% of people 12 and over have used illegal drugs or misused prescription drugs within the last year. If alcohol and tobacco are included, 165 million or 60.3% Americans ages 12 and older currently abuse drugs. Prevalence of alcohol use disorder (AUD) according to 2021 data shows 29.5 million people 12 and older (10.6 %) have AUD in 2021. Key findings indicate 50.9 %, half of people 12 and older have used an illicit drug at least once. 700,000 drug overdose deaths in the U.S. since 2000 are nearing a million. The federal budget for drug control in 2020 was $35 billion. (see Substance Abuse and Mental Health Services Administration -SAMHSA.gov>mental health for detailed statistics). The main problem in modern society is that we look for immediate gratification or a quick fix to our deep-down problems. We try to fix our internal imbalance with external substances like alcohol, drugs, chocolate, cheesecake, or video games. Commonly used drugs are tobacco, alcohol, marijuana, and opiates.

Tobacco Use

Smoking causes cancer, heart disease, strokes, lung disease, diabetes, and chronic obstructive pulmonary disease (COPD). 480,000 deaths per year, including 41,000 deaths resulting from secondhand smoke. Cigarette smoking remains the leading cause of preventable disease, disability, and deaths in the U.S. E-cigarette aerosol can contain acrolein, an herbicide primarily used to kill weeds. One puff can contain about as much nicotine as two packs of cigarettes. E-cigarette harmful agents like formaldehyde, acrolein, and acetaldehyde are all harmful and can lead to respiratory damage. Studies show nicotine in vaping products makes it even harder to quit.

Alcohol Use

It is estimated that more than 140,000 people (approximately 97,000 men and 43,000 women) die from alcohol related causes annually, making alcohol the fourth leading cause of death in the U.S, behind tobacco, poor diet and physical inactivity, and illegal drug use.

Marijuana Use

Marijuana, commonly called cannabis, is the most commonly used federally illegal drug in the United States, with an estimated 48.2 million, or about 18 % of Americans, using it at least once in 2019. Frequent use of cannabis can contribute to dependency on this substance. Frequent use of cannabis is related to anxiety and depression, and in the long term, use can harm important aspects of thinking, like learning and memory. There is a health risk associated with cannabis during pregnancy and breastfeeding. Close to 1 in 10 adults who use cannabis will become addicted. Medical use of cannabis for epilepsy, nausea, vomiting associated with cancer chemotherapy, and loss of appetite is permitted in some states in the United States. However, the recreational use of cannabis or any other illegal drugs should be discouraged due to health risks.

Opioid use

Opioid use disorder and opioid addiction remain at epidemic levels in the U.S and worldwide. Three million U.S. citizens currently suffer from opioid use disorder (OUD). More than 500,000 in the U.S. are dependent on heroin. Since 1999, the number of overdose deaths involving opioids (including prescription opioids) has quadrupled from 2000 to 2015, and more than half a million people have died from drug overdoses. And the CDC further indicates that 91 Americans die every day from an opioid overdose. Part of the problem with the opioid crisis is the prescription of OxyContin (opioids). One newspaper reported that one doctor in Florida had prescribed more opioids in three months than all the doctors combined in the whole year in California. Finally, that doctor was apprehended and served time in jail. Physicians in the U.S. frequently prescribe opioids to patients complaining of pain. There is nothing wrong with prescribing opioids to a patient after surgery or suffering from severe pain due to a serious medical condition to relieve pain. But it is a myth that patients will suffer pain significantly if not given OxyContin or opioids. In the Florida Department of Corrections, no inmate is given opioids, and there have not been any serious health issues reported in the media because opioids have not been given to inmates when they complain of severe pain. Lesser powerful pain medication is utilized in the prison system. Being a mental health and addiction professional, I have come across horrifying accounts and harm caused by addictive behaviors. In one instance, this individual narrated his downfall due to opioid addiction. He informed this therapist that one of his close friends died of an opioid overdose. His brother sold the family TV to buy heroin to support his drug habit. He himself had been incarcerated due to heroin use. Finally, he was placed on methadone treatment and court-ordered to receive counseling. In another case, another patient came to this therapist's office due to OxyContin overuse. He would go "doctor shopping" to get more OxyContin prescriptions as he was getting dependent on this drug. His wife found out and kicked him out of their house. Finally, he agreed to seek family counseling. This therapist wanted his wife to take control of dispensing the prescribed OxyContin as the doctor advised.

Drug-related problems contribute to more than 15% of hospital admissions. Adverse drug events contribute to 22.7 million hospitalizations in the U.S. annually, with 106,000 deaths. Dr. Mark Pitstick, in his book "Balanced Living," states that 1.5 million Americans are hospitalized and 100,000 die annually from prescription drug reactions. Deepak Chopra states that 80% of all drugs in Western medicine are optional or of marginal benefit. Coexisting addictions such as drug and alcohol, gambling, food, sex, internet, and gaming can become chronic and progressive if left unidentified and uncontrolled.

Group therapy is an excellent place to work with an addiction problem because it gives individuals a chance to receive feedback, to be confronted, learn useful information, and watch other people effectively or ineffectively deal with their problems. Individual therapy is only provided if used in conjunction with group therapy to focus on certain specific, unique problems and issues. Cognitive restructuring is an excellent technique to confront maladaptive behavior. It is based on the fact that thoughts cause feelings and feelings cause behavior. Changing misperceptions, stereotype beliefs, and cognitive distortions often lead to maladaptive functioning. Cognitive restructuring involves the identification of those thoughts that cause a negative emotional state and mal-adaptiveness and replacing them with healthier ways of thinking. Social skills training, such as effective communications, assertiveness training, stress and anger management, and other pertinent issues, are, incorporated into counseling sessions. Covert sensitization is an aversive counterconditioning procedure in which undesired behavior is paired with imagined scenes aversive to the patient in an attempt to eliminate unwanted behavior. Twelve-step programs are powerful peer support groups that help people recover from substance use disorder and behavioral addiction. Support groups such as alcoholic anonymous and Narcotics Anonymous serve as an adjunct to formal treatment as a form of common support group.

This clinician has designed a "Dual Diagnosis Program" to help individuals overcome their mental health and substance abuse problems. The program integrates chemical dependency and behavioral health treatment, focusing on didactic group therapy using structured sessions. The first session involves a clinical interview, mental status examination, administration of the substance abuse inventory, a structured clinical interview for DSM-5 disorder, and assessment of dual diagnosis.

Group sessions include the effects of dual disorders on life and understanding the mental health and addictive disorders, alcohol and drug history, and the medical and psychiatric effects of drugs and alcohol. Denial of addiction and psychiatric illness, road block to recovery for substance use, building emotional strength, coping with anger and anxiety, coping with boredom and depression, building relationship and support, developing relapse prevention, NA and mental health support group, changing and developing self -defeating behaviors, changing irrational beliefs, developing spirituality, making life style changes setting goals, preventing relapse, crisis intervention and writing down recovery plan.

The achievement of stable abstinence, the primary goal of the cessation regimen, is a necessary preparation for long-term treatment.

Improving Mental/Emotional Well-Being

Pertinent issues to improve mental/emotional well-being are: stress, anxiety, and anger management, effective communications/social skills, work-life balance, developing intimacy, innate needs, and achieving happiness.

Stress, Anxiety, and Anger Management

Facts about Stress- Seventy percent of the general population experience physical symptoms of stress, including headaches, tiredness, or sleeping problems. Eighty percent of U.S. workers say they experience stress on the job. Nearly half of U.S. adults (49%) say that stress has negatively affected their behavior. Sixty-five percent of Americans said that the current uncertainty in the nation causes their stress. It is estimated that job stress costs U.S. industry more than $300 billion a year in absenteeism, turnover, diminished productivity, medical, legal, and insurance costs. Stress is a common risk factor for 75-90% diseases, including the diseases that cause the foremost morbidity and mortality. According to the CDC/ National Institute on Occupational Safety and Health, the workplace is the number one cause of stress. The American Institute of Stress reports that 720,000 people die every year as a direct result of work-related stress.

Stress is the process of adjusting to circumstances that disrupt or threaten to disrupt a person's daily functioning. Stress is an automatic physical reaction to a change or demand. Muscles tighten, blood pressure rises, and the heart speeds up. Extra adrenaline rushes through your system. This reaction is an old-age survival response. Its purpose is to give the body extra strength needed to fight off danger or flee from it. Everyone feels stress. Stress is a part of life, and some stress can be good for you.

Eustress: Positive stress that inspires you to better meet life challenges. But too much stress can harm your physical and mental well-being. That is when it becomes distress.

Distress is the scientific term for excessive or undesired stress. During stress, sexual drive decreases in both sexes. Females are less likely to ovulate or carry a pregnancy to term, while males begin to have trouble with erections and secrete less testosterone. Long-term exposure to stress hormones leads to high blood pressure and atherosclerosis caused by the buildup of fatty deposits on the inner lining of the arteries. All of this increases the risk of a heart attack or stroke.

Physical Symptoms of Stress

Cardiovascular system- Heart pounding, cold, sweaty hands, headaches. Respiratory system- Shallow breathing, shortness of breath, asthma attack, and difficulties in speaking. Gastrointestinal symptoms- Upset stomach, diarrhea, abdominal pain. Muscular symptoms- Headaches, back or shoulder pain, arthritis. Skin Symptoms- acne, dandruff, dry skin. Immune symptoms- Allergy flare-up, catching a cold, and skin rash.

Emotional stress response- Emotional reactions include fear, anger, and frustration. In most cases, emotional stress reaction diminishes soon after the stressors are gone. However, if stressors continue for a long time, the emotional stress reaction may persist. When people do not have a chance to recover their emotional equilibrium, they feel tense, irritable, short-tempered, or anxious, and they may experience increasingly intense feelings of fatigue, depression, and hopelessness.

Cognitive stress response- Reduction in the ability to concentrate, to think clearly, or to remember accurately are typical cognitive stress reactions. Stress may also impair decision-making. Under stress, people who normally consider all aspects of situations before making a decision may act impulsively and sometimes foolishly.

Behavioral responses- Clues about people's physical and emotional stress reactions come from changes in how they look, act, or talk. Strained facial expression, a shaky voice, tremors, and jumpiness are common behavioral stress responses. Posture can also convey information about stress. Even more obvious behavioral stress responses occur as people attempt to escape or avoid stressors. Some people quit their jobs, drop out of school, turn to alcohol, or even attempt suicide. Aggression is another common behavioral response to stressors.

Linking Stress and Psychological Disorders

Physical, psychological, and behavioral responses sometimes appear together in a pattern known as burnout and post-traumatic stress disorder. Burnout is a pattern of physical, psychological, and behavioral dysfunction in response to continuous stressors. As burnout nears, previous reliable workers or once attentive spouses behave differently, disengaged, impulsive, or become accident-prone. They miss work frequently, oversleep, perform their task poorly, abuse alcohol or other drugs, and become irritable, suspicious, withdrawn, and depressed. Burnout accounts for some eleven percent of occupational disease claims made by U.S. workers. Post-traumatic stress disorder (PTSD) is a pattern of adverse reaction following a traumatic event, commonly involving reexperiencing of the events through nightmares or vivid memories. In some cases, flashbacks occur as if the trauma were occurring again.

Workplace stress- Major stressors in the workplace are overload, time pressure, organizational and personal change, technology, career challenges, and conflicts.

Overload- Overload occurs when the requirements of a job are greater than the ability of the worker. Time- pressure- customer demand speed and quality, and the competitive organization must deliver on both. As employees become more involved, they too will recognize the priority that time has in the workplace. The time factor, though, is a great stressor. Organizational and personal change- Change may include downsizing, new plant development, restricting work, new product development, changes in the pay system, corporate "buy-out", and many other organizational transitions. Many of these changes accompany the threat of job loss for many employees.

Technology- Robotics, computers, fax machines, and video displays all have their stressors. Learning about the machines that carry out work means acquiring skills to run and repair them.

Career challenges- The workforce is becoming more diversified. Jobs and careers are getting scarcer. For the person who has determined to rise through an organization, the challenge has recently become greater.

Conflict is largely responsible for emotional expressions at work. Conflicts have many forms, the most obvious being that between coworkers. However, conflict can arise between supervisor and subordinate as well. Another conflict that has a major effect on work is that of conflict from home.

Stress, the Immune system, and illness

The body's first line of defense against invading substances and microorganisms is the immune system. Psycho neuro immunology is the field that examines the interaction of psychological and physiological processes that alter the body's ability to defend itself against disease. Research has convincingly demonstrated that people under stress are more likely to develop infectious diseases than their less stressed counterparts.

Heart Disease and behavior pattern- A number of stress responses, especially anger and hostility, have been linked to coronary heart disease (CHD), particularly in men. CHD is a narrowing of a blood vessel that carries oxygen and nutrients to the heart muscles. Stress is one of the major factors contributing to CHD.

Stress and personality

Those who seem to be most hard-driven, restless, competitive, impatient, time-conscious, and quick to anger are classified as having a type A personality. Type A walks fast, talks fast, speeds through yellow traffic lights, gets easily angry at people who are late, works late at night, gets impatient, lashes out at others in frustration, and strives to win at all costs. On the other hand, type B are easy-going and laid back. Research has shown that Type A has an increased risk of CHD.

Stress Management

The technique useful for stress management is hardiness. It consists of 3Cs: commitment, control, and challenge. Commitment means personal commitment to work and personal life. It is the opposite of alienation and withdrawal. Control-you can influence events in your life. Act on the belief-opposite to helplessness, Challenge- view demands as challenging rather than a threat. Change is an opportunity. Challenges are positive and invigorating, while threats are negative and stressful. Research confirms that hardy people seem to be unusually resistant to stress.

Other ways to manage stress include relaxation techniques such as deep breathing, body scan, progressive muscle relaxation, biofeedback, meditation, guided imagery, cognitive reappraisal, social support system, and adequate sleep. These methods are also helpful in relieving and managing anxiety. These topics will be explored further under stress, anxiety, and anger management/ treatments.

Anger management

Anger is a normal human emotion. However, it is a secondary emotion. Typically, we experience a primary emotion like fear, loss, or sadness. Because these emotions create feelings of vulnerability and loss of control, they make us uncomfortable. One way of attempting to deal with these feelings is by subconsciously shifting into anger. Unlike fear and sadness, anger provides a sense of energy and makes us feel powerful and in charge rather than vulnerable and helpless. The downside of anger is that it can destroy relationships, tear apart families, and literally ruin a person's life when it is out of control. Anger is a strong feeling of annoyance and displeasure or hostility due to the perception of injustice and misdeeds, and attribution of blame that work together to fuel and fire the anger reaction. Anger can be a good thing. It can give you a way to express negative feelings or motivate you to find a solution to a problem. But excessive anger can cause increased blood pressure and other physical changes associated with anger, and make it difficult to think straight, harming your physical and mental health.

Three essential components of anger reaction are physiological, cognitive, and behavioral. **Physiological-** The area of the brain, the amygdala, mediates anger experiences, judging events as either aversive or rewarding. Neurotransmitter surge arouses the body. The physical sensation increases the heart rate, pulse rate, shallow, quick breathing, flushed skin, and an increase in muscle tension.

Cognitive- The way we perceive an event will eventually determine how we react to that event. A biased way of judging an event, as well as an unreasonable appraisal, can exacerbate or even create the perception of threat and provocation.

Behavioral- Two types of anger are anger-in and anger-out. Anger is a feeling of anger, but directed at /towards oneself, inwardly. It is manifested by depression or suppressed hostility. This harms the person experiencing anger-in. Anger out is a feeling of anger directed towards another person or things. This is outwardly directed anger. This harms others.

Anger is a feeling that needs to be vented without hostility or aggression. The consequences of inappropriate expression of anger can be very devastating. Anger is a problem when it is too frequent, lasts too long, leads to aggression, and disturbs work or relationships. Causes of anger are frustration, annoyance, harassment, hurt, disappointment, and threats. A person who feels a deep sense of inadequacy responds either aggressively or depressively, directing destructive anger outwards or inwards. Aggression is the response of an individual who externalizes the anger.

Road rage is a violent anger caused by the stress and frustration involved in driving a motor vehicle in difficult condition. Studies show that 82% of the drivers in the U.S. admit to having road rage or driving aggressively at least once in past year. 59% of drivers reported showing anger by honking, 45% drivers reported changing lanes without signaling. In 2022, someone was shot and killed every 16 hours. 66% of traffic fatalities are caused by aggressive driving.

In one of the anger management workshop conducted by this therapist, road rage story in the newspaper was narrated. A white guy cut off the other driver who was black. The other driver's six- year- old daughter was riding in the back seat of the car. The black driver tried to chase the white driver and both drivers were then cutting each other path. Finally, the white driver called his relative who showed up when both drivers were verbally confronting the other. The relative of the white driver shot through the window of the black driver car and a six -year-old daughter was killed. When I finished narrating this tragic road rage story, one of the person attending the workshop told this therapist that the black driver mentioned in this tragic episode was his boss and to this day he regrets chasing the other driver and losing his only child. It is unfortunate that anger out(aggression) has taken a heavy toll on this person's life.

This is another instance when individual sought therapy for anger problem. This person told this therapist that he is carrying the anger inside for last ten years after divorce from his wife. When this therapist asked the person what kind of feelings he has for his former wife. He told me that "she is a bitch'. After realizing that he had been carrying out this strong negative emotions for last ten years, I made him realize that he is suffering himself by keeping strong feelings of anger inside, even when his wife is not around him anymore. Even when his former wife did not care about him during marriage, he can at least care about himself. He can be good to himself by letting go the negative feelings he is having inside. Further when I inquired if anything good happened during his marriage. He informed me that he has two wonderful children whom he adores. By making him realize that he is blessed that his wife bore him these two precious children, his intensity of his dissipated.

In psychotherapy, we call this phenomen0on cognitive restructuring. This and other clinical tools will be described further in the stress, anxiety and anger treatments. In the anger management program developed by this therapist, the techniques to manage anger appropriately are: first to recognize that you have anger problem, identifying the causes of your anger and taking steps to manage anger through calming down, understanding your motives for anger and utilizing assertiveness instead of being either passive or aggressive.

Venting out anger without identifying the cause may feel good for a moment or two, but often cause us to behave in ways we regret later and seldom helps to address the underlying issues fueling the anger. Some of the appropriate steps to deal with anger effectively are:

1. Take time out- Stop, step back. Take a deep breath. Count up to 10. Counting up to 10 gives you time to calm down, so that you can think more clearly and overcome the impulses to lash out. Once you have calmed down, the chemicals within your body that are preparing you to fight dissipate, and your clear thinking comes back. With a calm mind, you are more likely to think rationally rather than act out impulsively.

2. Work out the problem- Anger tells you a problem exists: Take time to work out a solution to the problem. Unless the underlying issues are resolved, you will continue to find anger popping up. Anger alerts you to problems in your life so you can effectively solve them and build the life you desire.

3. Two common ways people deal with anger are through anger in and anger out. Keeping anger in and becoming passive causes depression, anxiety, and hostility. It is harmful to your physical and mental health. Anger out causes aggression. It will ruin your relationship with others. At extremes, verbal aggression causes feelings of hurt to others, and physical aggression can cause legal troubles for you. So, expressing anger without holding it in or lashing out is the appropriate step.

4. Between passive and aggression is assertiveness. In assertiveness, you express feelings of legitimate rights straightforwardly without attacking others or violating their rights. In assertiveness, you use the word "I" and in aggressiveness, you use the word "You". When you point a finger and blame the other person, the other person most likely will

do the same. Studies have shown that "I" statements reduce hostility and defensiveness, and "You" statements can provoke anger. The "I-ness" can help you communicate your concerns, feelings, and needs without blaming others or sounding threatening. It helps you get your point across; you statement tends to escalate conflicts.

5. Other tools to control flaring temper are humor, problem-solving, and physical activity. Physical exercise helps you reduce anxiety and calm you.

Some of the famous quotes on anger are:

Holding on to anger is like grasping a hot coal with the intent of throwing it at someone else; you are the one who gets burned. --Buddha

You will not be punished for your anger; you will be punished by your anger- Buddha

Anyone can become angry-that is easy, but to be angry with the right person, and to the right degree, and at the right time, and for the right purpose, and the right way-and that is not easy-Aristotle.

For every minute you remain angry, you give up sixty seconds of peace of mind- Ralph Waldo Emerson.

Finally, as someone said, when anger is so much a part of your personality that you lose the capacity to find peace, it is an indication that your good beliefs are ironically working against you.

Treatment for Stress, Anxiety, and Anger

Effective techniques to manage stress, anxiety, and anger are relaxation methods, cognitive reappraisal, a social support system, humor, and adequate sleep.

Relaxation methods include deep breathing, alternative nostril breathing (topics covered under complete yoga breath), progressive muscle relaxation, body scan, relaxation imagery, biofeedback, and yoga techniques, including meditation and mindfulness.

Progressive muscle relaxation (PMR)- It is important to realize that relaxation is a skill. In progressive muscle relaxation (PMR), you learn how to gain control over feelings of tension and anxiety, to enjoy more comfortable feelings of deep relaxation. PMR works by teaching the person to identify the feelings of muscle relaxation and to recognize how those feelings are different from muscular tension. This is done through a series of exercises that involve tensing and relaxing the muscle groups. Worrying automatically tenses the muscles, and relaxing the muscles relieves tense feelings. The method involves first tightening and relaxing the muscles throughout your body. First, you create tension in the muscle group, making the muscle as tight as possible without creating any pain or cramps. This tightness is held for 5 to 7 seconds while you pay attention to how the tension feels. Then you relax the muscle group. Let the muscle become totally loose, letting go of all possible tension. The relaxation stage should last about 15 seconds. Then you repeat the procedure: (a) tense the muscle group, (b) hold the tension and study it for 5 to 7 seconds, then(c) relax the muscles, letting the tension go and noticing the difference in feelings. Through this method, you can eventually learn conscious control over your muscles, without having to use the tensing exercise.

Lie down on your back in a comfortable place, such as an exercise mat. Close your eyes if you wish. The muscle groups in this order for practicing this exercise.

1. Hands- Tighten your right hand by making a fist and squeezing. Then relax.
2. Forearms and back of hands- Bend your right hand at the wrist, pointing your fingers straight up towards the ceiling. Study the tension. Then relax your right hand. Study the feelings when these muscles relax.
3. Biceps- flex the large muscle in your upper arm by touching your right arm to your shoulder, tensing the large biceps muscles. Then relax. Before going on, take time to compare the feelings in your right and left arms and hands. Then repeat steps 1-3 with the left hand and arm.
4. Shoulders- Bring your shoulders up, as if you were touching your ears with them. Then relax.
5. Forehead- Wrinkle up your forehead, raising your eyebrows as far as they will go. Study the tension back across your scalp. Then relax.
6. Upper face- Squint your eyes very tightly, and wrinkle up your nose. Then relax.
7. Lips and jaws- press your lips together, and clinch your teeth to create tension in your jaws. Not too hard: you can damage your teeth. Then relax.
8. Tongue and throat- Press your tongue into the roof of your mouth, and relax.
9. Neck muscle-Bend your chin towards your chest. Then relax.

10. Chest- Take a deep breath and hold it. Then let it out quickly. Try it again, exhaling slowly this time. Feel the relaxation.

11. Back- arch your back> Arch slightly, being careful not to strain or tense the muscle too hard. Then relax.

12. Stomach- Squeeze your abdominal muscles tight. Then relax.

13. Buttocks- Tighten your buttock muscles, feeling your pelvis up slightly. Then relax.

14. Thighs- lift your legs straight out, holding them off the floor, creating tension in your thighs and perhaps in your stomach and back, and then relax.

15. Calves- Point your toes back towards your head, creating tension in your calves, then relax.

16. Feet- curl your toes downwards, as if digging them into the sand. Then relax.

When you have finished this, notice how you feel all over your body. Do a mental check of each part of your body, letting go of any tension that remains. If any part of your body seems tense, go back and repeat the tightening-relaxing exercise for that part. Now allow your body to remain relaxed. Let yourself feel very loose, very light. Learn to breathe as you do when you are asleep; by taking a deep but comfortable breath, exhaling it gradually, and then pausing while your breath is out.

Body Scan- This exercise will help you become more aware of how you are feeling right now. As you become aware of your body, mind, and emotions in a nonjudgmental way, you will begin to experience a new clarity and acceptance that will help you relax deeply. Do your best not to judge yourself as you are doing this exercise. Get into a comfortable position, either sitting up or lying down, where you won't be disturbed. Gently close your eyes and focus your complete attention on your breathing, cool air being breathed in, warm air being breathed out. Just breathe naturally. Noticing each breath. Suppose your mind strays away from your breath. With thoughts about something else, just bring your focus gently back to your breath.

Focus your attention on different parts of your body, toes, feet, legs, knees, upper part of legs, buttocks, lower abdomen, stomach, chest, back, hands, arms, shoulders, neck, mouth, nose, face, and head. Are you experiencing any tightness or discomfort in these areas? Completely feel whatever you are feeling. Then simply and completely let it go. Notice the relaxation as it penetrates every organ, every muscle, and every cell of your body. Let your whole body and mind completely relax. Enjoy the feelings of deep relaxation.

Relaxation Imagery

Another valuable tool in combating stress is to conjure a peaceful, relaxing scene. The idea is to think about, and visualize in detail, a time and place where you have felt especially safe, secure, and perfectly at peace. It sometimes helps to begin the process by imagining that you are walking down a path, and come to a meadow. Here is a peaceful clearing, where the sun is always shining, warming your skin, and the grass smells lush. You can hear the tinkling of a brook nearby. Perhaps it is this meadow that you were looking for, or you may want to follow the road leading to the beach, where the waves come and go, caressing the white sand. The salty smell in the air clears your mind, and the sound of the waves lulls you into a peaceful state, or you can see in the distance a cottage tucked into the side of a hill, with smoke lazily rising from the chimney. It is cozy in front of the fireplace. The smell of your favorite soup wafts from the kitchen and permeates the air, bringing back warm, nurturing memories.

Now it is time to create your own personal relaxation image. Perhaps one of the scenarios above triggered a memory for you. Or maybe a memorable, pleasant moment of your childhood will work for you. Bring it slowly, with your eyes closed, sketching it in broad strokes like an artist sketching on a canvas. Relaxation imagery may be used in conjunction with progressive muscle relaxation and body scan to experience deep relaxation.

Biofeedback is a type of mind-body technique you use to control some of your body's functions, such as your heart rate, breathing patterns, and muscle responses. During a body feedback session, a certified health care provider places painless sensors or devices on your body. The sensors measure physiological signals from your body, such as breathing rate and patterns with bands around your stomach and chest, heart rate with a pulsometer sensor connected to electrocardiogram (EKG), muscle movement and tension using surface electromyography (EMG), sweat with galvanic skin response (GSR), usually attached to your finger tip and/or palm, electric beam activity using electroencephalogram (EEG) which involves sensors attached to your scalp. EEG feedback is also called neurofeedback. Skin temperature with a skin sensor.

Computers process the information from these sensors or devices and quickly report it back to you. As you receive the feedback, your provider will suggest strategies to change how your body is functioning. Your provider may suggest how you can change your breathing pattern to calm anxiety and lower your heart rate, or you may be given suggestions on how to relax.

Yoga and Mental Health

Fifth, sixth, seventh, and eighth limbs of yoga are Pratyahara (sense withdrawal), Dharana (concentration), Dhyana (meditation), and Samadhi (contemplation, absorption, or super consciousness). These limbs of yoga facilitate a calm and serene mind and improve focus.

Pratyahara is the withdrawal of the senses to still the mind. When the mind gains control over the senses, distraction from outside lessens, and the mind can turn inward and focus on the other limbs of yoga. Pratyahara asks us to let go of life's distractions. You can do this by reducing social media time or meditating for 20 minutes. The practice of *pratyahara* provides us with an opportunity to step back and take a look at ourselves. This withdrawal allows us to objectively observe our cravings: habits that are perhaps detrimental to our health and which likely interfere with our inner growth.

Dharna is a state of no distraction. Having relieved ourselves of outside distraction, we can now deal with the distraction of mind itself. In the practice of concentration, which precedes meditation, we engage our thinking process by concentrating on a single object.

Dhayana is a meditation. Meditation is a state of pure thought and absorption in the object of meditation. To achieve the state of lasting happiness and absolute peace, we must first know how to calm the mind, concentrate, and go beyond by turning the concentration inwards, upon the self. We can deepen that experience of perfect concentration. Meditation and mindful practice are being described in detail in the next section.

Samadhi is a state of super consciousness. In *Samadhi,* non-duality or oneness is experienced. At this stage, the meditator merges with his or her point of focus and transcends the self altogether. The meditator comes to realize a profound connection to the divine, interconnected with all living things. If we pause to experience what we really want to get out of life, would not joy, fulfillment, and freedom somehow find their way into our list of hopes, wishes, and desires? Completion of the yoga path is what, deep down, all human beings aspire to. The ultimate stage of yoga practice will lead us to enlightenment, inner peace, and joy.

Meditation and Mindfulness- Word meditation comes from the Sanskrit word *medha,* which can be translated as "doing" the wisdom. People who meditate for spiritual purposes typically do some focused deep breathing first to get into a calm, receptive frame of mind. This, while still in the meditative state, they reflect on a certain experience or issue. Meditation focuses your mind intently on a particular thing or activity. At the same time, being relatively oblivious to everything else. Meditation is centered around slow, steady breathing and a non-judgmental focus on the present moment. By reducing anxiety and rumination, it has been found to have sweeping health benefits, including the ability to help reduce insomnia. To start meditation, follow these simple steps.

1. Focus on slowly inhaling and exhaling at a comfortable pace.
2. Notice the position of your body.
3. Notice any sensation in your body.
4. Focus on your breath.
5. Count to 4 slowly as you inhale.
6. Count to 6 slowly as you exhale.

Continue this process for 10 to 15 minutes for a meditation session. You can choose to meditate on anything that appeals to you. Gazing at the object, such as a candle flame or a favorite picture, will focus your attention, or you may choose to repeat either loud or to yourself, a syllable. Words like "AUM (a Sanskrit word symbolizing the universe).

Meditation is the best practice to develop self-control and willpower, bring the mind and body into focus, and control. Researchers have shown that meditation can produce changes in immune function and blood pressure that may have important implications for health. Meditation has also been shown to improve the quality of life for people with a wide range of medical conditions, including breast cancer, prostate cancer, psoriasis, chronic pain, and anxiety disorders.

Mindfulness is paying attention to one's ongoing experience in a way that allows openness, fully present and aware, during our daily activities. Stop and smell the roses is a reminder that one must pay attention to the journey as well as goals. Get involved in the activities that are personally meaningful. Mindfulness, in conjunction with meditation and deep breathing (described under Yoga breath), can help decrease anxiety. It can also help relieve symptoms of stress, anxiety, anger, exhaustion, and depression, as well as improve quality of life. Further deep breathing releases chemicals, such as endorphins. Deep breathing increases the flow to your major muscles.

Progressive muscle relaxation, body scan, relaxation imagery, meditation, mindfulness, and yoga practices are a holistic way to reduce anxiety, reduce symptoms of stress, exhaustion, and depression, and improve quality of life.

Cognitive restructuring will be discussed at the end of this section, as it has broad application to help you get a grip on many facets of life.

Social Support System

Human connection is a fundamental aspect of well-being, offering support, belonging, and a sense of community. Everyone needs good family and friends or supporters whom you can call on when you need to talk or you can count on in times of need. Choose people whom you love and trust. Choose the one who can sympathize, affirm your individuality and your strength, who is open-minded, accepts your ups and downs without being judgmental. And work with you as you decide your best step, and support you as you carry through. Specialized support groups include alcoholics anonymous, narcotics anonymous, cancer, bereavement, or caregiving. Support groups bring together people who are going through or have gone through similar experiences. When my dear mother was diagnosed with terminal cancer, the cancer support group helped me cope with the difficult time in my life. Studies have shown that persons with good family and friends support, and a social support system, result in enhanced mental health, sense of belonging, and better self-esteem.

Humor

Humor is yet another powerful strategy. Humor is, at its core, an expression of joy, optimism, and a positive outlook. Studies have shown physiological evidence for humor's stress-busting capacity. Researchers have found that "mirthful laughter"-in other words, happy laughter as opposed to black humor or sarcasm can reduce stress hormones and enhance immune function. At the same time, humor also combats stress on a psychological level by changing people's perception of events. Think about all the times you have seen an argument averted because someone cracked a joke to diffuse a tense situation. When you are afraid, humor can knock a perceived threat down to a more manageable size. When you are depressed, a little levity can help you regain your perspective.

Effective Communication/ Social Skills

Effective communications and social skills are closely interconnected, with each other's skill set enhancing the other. Effective communications rely on social skills such as active listening, empathy, and assertiveness. At the same time, social skills are enhanced through effective communication. Speaking and listening are vital social skills. Our ability to listen to others and respond as required is crucial in communication with others. Your choice of words in any social setting must be in line with that particular context. Having an open mind allows us to pay attention to the nonverbal gestures. In my therapeutic practice, I always pay attention to nonverbal cues such as facial expression, voice tone, gestures, appearance, and posture to assess patients' feelings. Four main qualities for interpersonal skills are:

Sensitivity- Be aware of the different needs of each other.

Tolerance- set aside your personal beliefs so that you can objectively work with and understand the beliefs of the other person.

Assertion- Be assertive, but do not have to be arrogant to get your point across.

Restraint- you need to have the presence of mind to stop and think before speaking or taking action. Here is the list of essential social skills.

1. Problem-solving skills-Problem-solving skills are an essential part of our social skills. This is mainly because conflicts and disagreements will always come about as a result of our social interactions. Your ability to resolve conflicts will help you work well with others.

2. Communication skills- As stated earlier, speaking and listening are vital social skills. Our ability to listen to others and respond as required is crucial.

3. Be considerate and courteous- Be considerate of others or the situation, courtesy in interaction with others or through writing will enhance social relationships.

4. Curiosity and open-mindedness- Have an open mind and willingness to explore all possibilities or options. Entering into a conversation with a fixed mindset limits us from seeing other opportunities and ideas that can be exploited. Our level of curiosity and being open-minded are crucial social skills.

5. Be aware of your surroundings- Our social skills will be effective when we have a thorough understanding of our surroundings.

6. Stay Positive- Nobody wants to hang out with someone who is always complaining and negative. Regardless of your circumstances, try to be the kind of person who sees glass half full rather than half empty.

7. Accept Criticism- No need for defensiveness when critiqued. We are not perfect and make mistakes from time to time. Constructive criticism and feedback help us to improve ourselves.

Work-life Balance- Several statistics show that more than 60 percent of U.S. employees feel like their work-life balance is out of whack. With too many struggling to find harmony between their jobs and their home life, it can seem inevitable to feel overwhelmed and overworked.

A healthy work-life balance refers to maintaining a harmonious relationship between your work and personal life. It involves consciously managing your time and energy to meet both professional and personal commitments while prioritizing self-care and well-being. Some characteristics of a healthy work-life balance may include:

Set boundaries- Clear boundaries between work and personal life by defining specific working hours and separating work-related tasks from personal activities.

Time management- Efficiently organizing and prioritizing tasks, ensuring that you allocate enough time for work responsibilities as well as personal pursuits, such as spending time with family, engaging in hobbies, or pursuing personal goals.

Stress management- Implementing strategies to manage stress levels, such as practicing mindfulness, engaging in regular physical activity, taking breaks, and unplugging from work-related activities when needed.

Flexibility- Having the ability to adapt and adjust your schedule to accommodate personal needs without jeopardizing work commitments. Just like in our diets to stay healthy and energized for the long haul, people need variety; in the same way, when it comes to work-life balance, people need to engage in a variety of activities and rest.

Workaholics are those who struggle to practice self-care, find themselves at higher risk for neglected personal life, fatigue, and stress-related health issues.

Here are some of the tips to have a good work-life balance.

1. Plan ahead to combine work activities with leisure, social, or fitness activities.
2. Set blocks of time for check and response messages, a time to take meetings, and a time to do mentally intensive work.
3. Get out for lunch, or enjoy lunch with co-workers; the change of pace will be refreshing.
4. Take time off- Time off, including sick time, personal time, and vacations, is an important way to nourish your well-being.
5. Practice mindfulness- Mindfulness, like meditation, breath awareness, may help you to become more in tune with your emotional and physical sensations.
6. Find something you love outside of work to engage in our hobbies, to burst our energy and vitality.
7. Recommend work that makes you yearn for balance. Find work that provides moments of satisfaction, accomplishments, and connection.
8. Work with a coach or therapist- if you are overwhelmed, stuck, or don't know where to begin to disconnect, working with a professional can be invaluable.

Building a strong relationship and intimacy

Trust, sincerity, mutual understanding, companionship, friendship, respect, similarity of attitude and value, reciprocity, mutual exchange of positive emotions, self-disclosure, warmth, dependability, and emotional stability contribute to intimacy. One of the main foundations of a healthy relationship is the ability to trust one another. Without trust, it is difficult to be truly intimate with another person. Trust is the basic confidence that you can share who you are with your partner, and that will be accepted and loved. It is the belief that your partner cares for you and that has your best interest at heart. Trust and sincerity go hand in hand. Mutual understanding and reassuring your partner that you love, accept, and appreciate your loved one unconditionally will improve intimacy.

There are three kinds of relationships. Dependent, independent, and interdependent. In a dependent relationship, each person needs the other for something. This relationship impedes autonomy, as your emotional growth is dependent on another person. You don't control your own life. This is a dysfunctional relationship. Another variant of this relationship is being codependent. Co-dependent persons feel worthless unless they are needed by and making drastic sacrifices for the enabler. The enabler gets satisfaction from getting their every need met by the other person.

An independent relationship can look like carving out alone time, having your own hobbies, and spending time with your own friends that cultivate a strong outside of the relationship. Functional marriage and relationships require a balance. There should be a balance between togetherness, individuality, and independence.

Interdependence suggests that partners recognize and value the importance of the emotional bond they share while maintaining a solid sense of self within the relationship dynamic, because it allows partners to be autonomous but also come together as a team. In an interdependent relationship, both partners have a sense of healthy autonomy.

In a close relationship. If one partner does not feel secure, then the partner can reassure the insecure person that he or she is valued and loved unconditionally. The following cases of my therapy session illustrate this point.

During the couple therapy session, the wife complained that her husband never compliments her. Husband responded by saying that he frequently says that she looks nice. The wife in the session stated that her husband should use word nice for their son. He should tell her that "she looks sexy". Her husband does not realize his wife needs and perspective that she likes to be acknowledged, that she looks beautiful and sexy.

In another couple therapy session, the guy complained that his girlfriend does not like to take a shower with him. The girlfriend replied that she does not want his boyfriend to see her fat ass. In this instance, the girlfriend is very conscious of her weight, as most of the females in Western society are. The boyfriend replied that he likes his girlfriend's fat ass. I have heard many times that females complain that they have to be super thin to be considered beautiful and desirable. In that context, many females don't eat well and develop anorexia. Two important points to be considered here from a therapeutic perspective are that, first of all, we need to learn to accept ourselves as we are, and second, our loved ones also need to accept us unconditionally. Having said that, maintaining good health is important, but not to become super thin to satisfy your partner or meet the Barbie doll standard. Nurturing cooperation, respect for the other person's needs is possible when a couple is willing to do so through active listening and confirmation that the interlocutor's message is understood. The way to success in this endeavor is for the couple to clearly articulate what they expect from themselves, from their other spouse, and from their relationship so that it can function effectively.

Feeling of Love

The quality of our social relationships is one of the control factors of whether we feel content, satisfied, and happy with our lives. Intimacy and love are significant parts of enhancing our relationships with loved ones.

Sternberg's Love Triangle

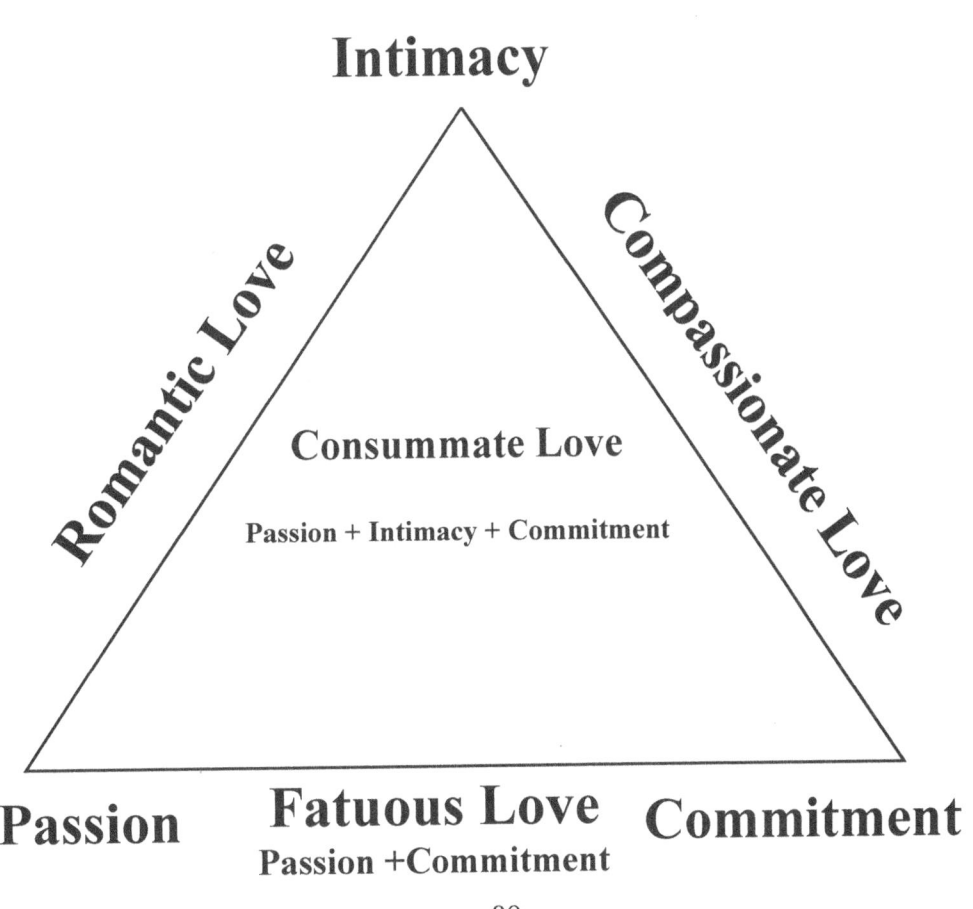

89

The Sternberg triangular theory of love holds that love can be understood in terms of three components that together can be viewed as forming the vertices of a triangle. These three components are passion, intimacy, and commitment. At the beginning, passion is very high, intimacy steadily increases throughout the relationship, and commitment may start slowly but increases over time. Passion refers to the drive that led to romance, physical attraction, sexual consummation in loving relationship. Intimacy refers to the feelings of closeness, connectedness, and bondedness in loving relationship. Commitment refers to the maintain the love in the long term. These three components of love interact with each other. Romantic love derives from combination of the passion and intimacy. Commitment love derives from combination of passion and commitment. Consummate, or complete love results from the full combination of all three components. This author has come up with his own version of AAA model of love as starting with attraction, move on to attachment, and then on to absorption. Initially there is physical attraction, then emotional attachment and then emerges with deep absorption in love.

New testament 1 Corrnthians13:4-8 gives beautiful definition of love as "love is patient and kind. Love dies not envy. Love does not brag, is not proud, doesn't behave itself inappropriately, doesn't seek its own way, is not provoked, takes no account of evil, doesn't rejoice in unrighteousness, but rejoices with the truth. Bears all things, believes all things, and endures all things. Love never fails".

Love is one of the important components of a fulfilling life. Before we love someone else, we need to start to love ourselves, accept ourselves as we are, and then move on to love someone else.

Maslow's Hierarchy of Innate Needs

Maslow delineated five basic human needs that must be met in order for people to feel fulfilled in life.

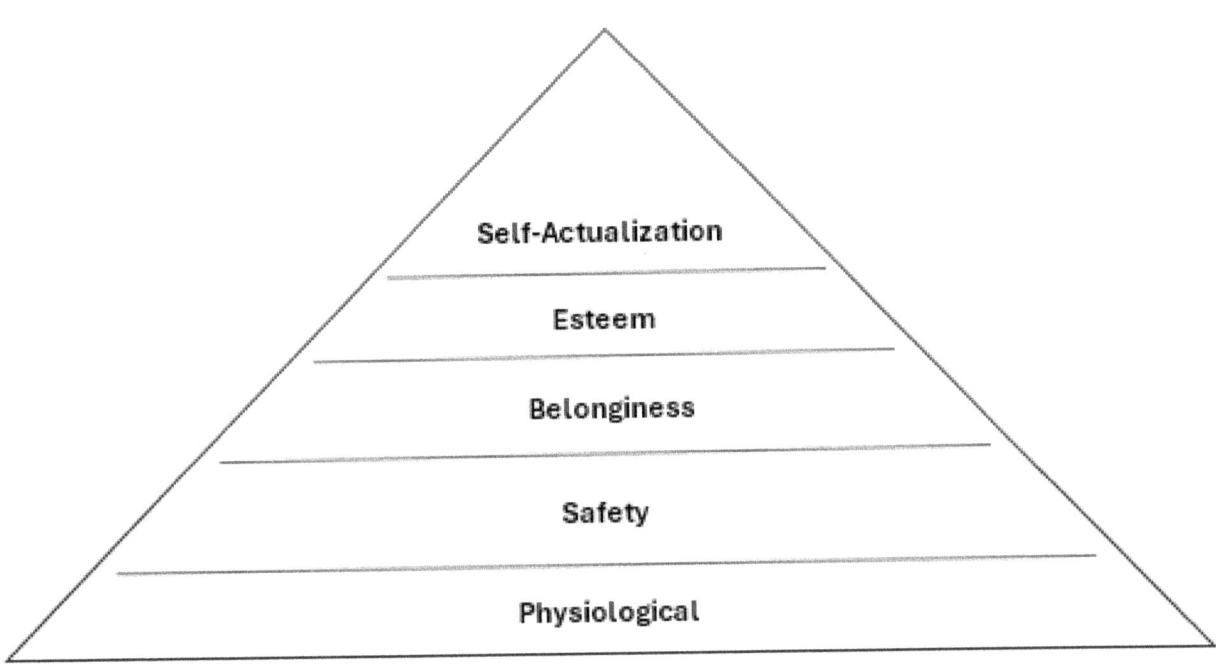

Maslow assumed these five needs to be innate

1. Physiological- Basic needs for food, shelter, comfort, and freedom from disease.
2. Safety and Security- safety from physical harm and societal chaos.
3. Love and Belongingness- Connection with the social world and the need to be loved and cherished.
4. Self-Esteem- need to feel a sense of competence and achievement, feelings of being viewed and respected by others.
5. Self-actualization- People have a need to develop their unique potentials.

Maslow stated that a person might have satisfied 85% of his physiological needs, 70% of safety needs, 50% of belongingness needs, 40% of self-esteem needs, and 10% of self-actualization needs. However, thirty percent of Americans gain the courage to continue living at the level of self-esteem and above. For those living predominantly in the self-actualized level, only one percent of Americans currently rise to that level to live "fully alive". We are selfish, or rather self-centered, on the basic level, but our selfishness disappears on the actualization level. Therefore, we are then able to give our all to others altruistically when we can live at the actualized level.

Peace is possible when you have good health and basic needs of food, shelter, and clothing, including a safe living environment. When you have a sense of belonging, you have a loving family, friends, and community. These are the basic hierarchy of needs. When you feel good about yourself, have self-worth, and you transcend to self-actualization, then you have joy or bliss. Maslow's personality traits of self-actualization are open to new experience, self-acceptance, acceptance of others, and open to joy, gratitude, creativity, autonomy, deep feelings of empathy, and authenticity.

In 1968, Maslow added a sixth need on top of his hierarchy, the need for transcendence or to expand one's sense of meaning in life through the development of a more spiritual perspective. Maslow came to believe that people need to connect with something larger than the individual self. Generally, in western society, most of the people have their basic needs, physiological, safety and security, and belongingness needs met to a significant degree. The problem starts with the esteem needs. Many people do not feel good about themselves. That is the root cause of problems in depression, anxiety, relationships, work, and overall well-being. Maslow's fourth hierarchy of needs is crucial in building self-confidence and self-worth.

This therapist, in his clinical practice, started a self-esteem program to help individuals build healthy self-esteem. The purpose of this program has been to help individuals trust their intuition, appreciate their special talents, and become capable, productive, and effective members of society. Individuals will learn to accept and value themselves, build self-confidence, and improve self-esteem. Healthy self-esteem is based on the ability to assess ourselves accurately (know ourselves) and to accept and value ourselves. That means being able to realistically acknowledge our strengths and limitations and at the same time accepting ourselves as worthy and worthwhile without conditions or reservations. Nathaniel Bradon, founder of the self-esteem movement, defines self-esteem as the disposition to experience ourselves as competent to cope with the challenges of life, as deserving of happiness. Competent comes from an internal locus of control or self-efficacy. Self-efficacy is the belief that we have the ability to perform /or the capacity to learn the behavior necessary to reach desired goals. The desired goals have to be realistic. The role of self-concept consists of three parts: ideal self, self-image, and self-esteem.

Self-esteem depends on the gap between

Ideal self and self-image. Therefore, self-esteem

Can be increased by raising the self-image,

Lowering the ideal self, or both.

```
┌─────────────────┐
│    Ideal-Self    │
│                  │
│         •        │
│                  │
│         •        │
│                  │
│         •        │
│                  │
│         •        │
│                  │
│   Self-Image     │
└─────────────────┘
```

First thing to build a self-image or self-esteem is to learn to accept your feelings in these areas.

Worth- Value placed on ourselves.

Example- I love and appreciate myself for who I am.

Feelings- How in touch are we?

Example- I listen to my feelings and respect them.

Focus-Ability to look at ourselves.

Example- I know that it is okay to take care of my needs.

Growth- Commitment to growth.

Example- I find each day challenging and exciting.

Nurturing- Care for self.

Example- I take good care of myself.

Guidance- Ability to set a course for our lives.

Example- I make decisions for myself.

Determinations- Commitment to ourselves.

Example- I am always ready to set new goals.

Healing- Ability to take care of our minds and bodies.

Example- I have the power to make myself feel good.

Love- Ability to love who we are.

Example- I love myself.

Steps to Build self-esteem

Identify and accept your limitations- To raise self-esteem, it is necessary to identify and accept your limitations. Becoming realistic about who you are and what you can and cannot do. Demanding perfection of yourself is unrealistic because no one is perfect. Acknowledge your mistakes, learn from them, and then move on. Your future, however, can be effectively shaped by how you think and act from this day on.

Take responsibility for your decisions- Making decisions for yourself helps you develop confidence in your judgement and enables you to explore options.

Develop expertise in some area- Developing "expert power" not only builds your self-esteem but also increases the value of your contribution to an organization. Identify and cultivate a skill or talent you have.

Set goals- Persons who consistently set goals are able to manage high self-esteem. People who fail to set goals wander aimlessly through life with no purpose, and they are more likely to suffer from low self-esteem.

Steps to achieve short-term goals are:

1. Start with a short-term goal.
2. Goal is something you desire.
3. Goal is attainable.
4. Goal is measurable.
5. Write it down.
6. Goal is under your control.
7. One goal at a time.

One of the significant processes in building self-esteem is to think positively about yourself by

1. Identify and accept your strengths.
2. Help yourself- Learn new skills, develop abilities.
3. Encouragement- "can do attitude.
4. Praise- Take pride in your achievement.
5. Time- Enjoy reading, crafts, etc.
6. Enjoy your company.
7. Trust- Pay attention to your thoughts and feelings.
8. Respect- Explore and appreciate your specific talents.
9. Love- learn to love the unique person you are,
10. Take pride in your individuality.

Last, but not least, to build self-esteem is to use positive self-talk. People with a strong inner critic will receive frequent negative messages that can erode their self-esteem. It helps to reject those messages with positive self-talk. To boost my own self-esteem, I have come up with this quote of mine.

"Do not let your limitations limit what you can do; use your strength to achieve the goals you want to pursue."

Happiness

There are two fundamental types of happiness, namely hedonism and eudaimonism. Hedonic happiness comes from the pursuit of pleasure and avoidance of pain, whereas eudaimonic happiness comes from the pursuit of authenticity, meaning, virtue, and growth.

Hedonia relates to immediate sensory pleasure, happiness and enjoyment. Anyone can experience hedonic pleasure just by having a delicious meal, wearing a beautiful-looking dress, watching a favorite team win, playing a video game, ingesting drugs, or having a pleasant sexual encounter. The problem with this kind of happiness is that it is just momentary. Pleasure is pleasant, beautiful, but it is enslaving. True happiness, or authentic happiness, which considers joy or bliss, is liberating.

True happiness is centered on finding positive emotions in life, meaning often involves recognizing and accepting both positive and negative emotions, accepting and integrating all emotions, and a profound connection with others. A quick glance at various social indices could lead one to conclude that unhappiness is rampant. News reports portray society with a rising rate of divorce, drug problems, and crime.

The six core variables that both predict happiness and satisfaction in life in Western industrialized culture are:

1. Positive self-esteem
2. Sense of perceived control
3. Extroversion
4. Optimism
5. Positive social relationship
6. A sense of meaning and purpose in life.

Positive self-esteem and sense of perceived control(self-efficacy) and positive social relationships have already been discussed. It is also found that extraverts enjoy and participate more in social activities, and happiness is correlated with extraversion, enjoyment, and participation in social activities. Optimism and having positivity will be discussed under cognitive restructuring. A sense of meaning and purpose in life is covered under spiritual health.

Authentic Happiness

Authenticity is finding one's true self, an honest self-examination. Authenticity involves both the ability to recognize and take responsibility for one's own psychological experiences and the ability to act in a way that is consistent with those experiences, as well as honest awareness of self.

Eudaimonia is a state or condition of "good spirit", and what is commonly translated as "happiness'. Eudaimonia is a state or condition of "good spirit', and which is commonly translated as "happiness". Eudaimonia is a much deeper and richer concept than happiness. It is more stable and cannot be quickly taken away from us.

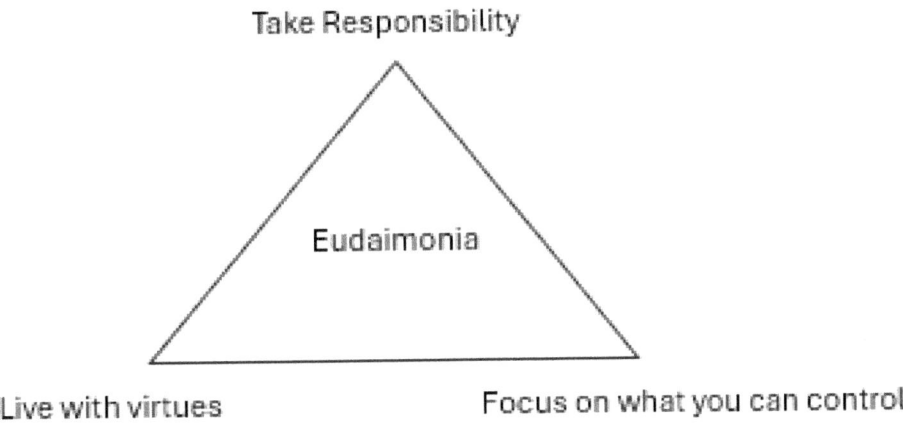

The Stoic triangle of happiness is a three-step model that focuses on living with virtues, self-control, and personal responsibility that blend together. This condition was "Eudaimonia". Eudaimonia is a term that comes from Aristotle's work called Nicomachean Ethics and means individual well-being and happiness. The prefix eu (meaning good) and daimon (spirit).

Maslow's fifth hierarchy of needs, self-actualization, and sixth level is intrinsic value or self-transcendence, which represents the drive to move beyond the self and individual concerns, and is connected with authenticity and eudaimonia. In Vedic culture, the term eudaimonia is equated with bliss, which is equivalent to superior happiness, utter joy, or contentment.

Authentic happiness is living in peace and harmony with your body, mind, and soul. Happiness is a consequence of your personal efforts and living a life of purpose. Some key signs of happiness include:

Feeling like you are living the life you wanted.

Willingness to take life as it comes.

Feeling that your life is good.

Enjoying a positive, healthy relationship with other people.

Being open to new ideas or experiences.

Practicing self-care and treating yourself with kindness and compassion.

Experiencing gratitude

Feeling that you are living with a sense of meaning and purpose and sharing your happiness and joy with others.

One important thing to remember is that happiness is not a state of constant euphoria. Instead, happiness is our overall sense of experience, a more positive emotion. Happy people still feel the whole range of human emotions, like frustration, boredom, loneliness, and even sadness from time to time. But when faced with discomfort, they have an underlying sense of optimism that things will get better, that they will be able to deal with what is happening, and that they will be able to feel happy again. Here are ways to cultivate happiness.

Pursue intrinsic goals- Achieving goals that you are intrinsically motivated to pursue, particularly those that are focused on personal growth and fulfillment.

Enjoy the moment- Practice gratitude for things you have and enjoy the process as you go.

Reframing negative thoughts- Reframing the negative perception is not about ignoring the bad; instead, it means trying to take a more balanced, realistic look at events.

Cultivate strong relationships- Social support is an essential part of well-being. Research has found that good social relationships are the strongest predictor of happiness.

Get regular exercise- Exercise is good for both your body and mind. Physical activity improves mood.

Show gratitude- Persons who show gratitude have increased positive emotions, increased subjective happiness, and improved life satisfaction.

Treatment of Mental Disorders

There are many types of therapeutic interventions to help individuals cope with their struggles and overcome difficult circumstances. This therapist's favorite approach to successfully counseling and helping his patients has been cognitive restructuring. Cognitive restructuring is a technique that has been successfully used to help people change the way they think. This technique comes from cognitive behavior therapy (CBT), which is a talk therapy that can help manage your problems by changing the way you think and behave. CBT is most commonly used to treat depression and anxiety. Another version of CBT or cognitive restructuring is rational emotive behavior therapy (REBT). This approach was developed by Dr. Albert Ellis in the 1950s. It is based on Epictetus, a first-century A.D. philosopher who said, "Men are disturbed not by the things, but by the views which they take of them". William Shakespeare said the same thing:" Nothing is good or bad, but thinking makes it so". REBT is an A, B, C, D model, where A is the activating event and C is the consequences. Between A and C is the B, belief system. Ellis stated that it is not the events that directly cause emotions and behaviors. Rather, it is one's belief about the events that lead to emotional and behavioral reactivity.

A	B	C
Activating event	Beliefs	consequences

REBT enables the patient to realize that it is not the outside events (A) that cause their dysfunctional reactions (C). It is their irrational beliefs (B), and they are in control of how they respond to adversity, because they can have autonomy over their beliefs. In REBT, besides A, B, and C, there is D, which stands for disputing irrational beliefs, and E is the result of the new, effective emotions resulting from more reasonable beliefs (thinking) about the original event. Here is a sample of a rational emotive behavior therapy scene.

A- activating event- The Teenage girl's first boyfriend broke up with her.

B- irrational belief-

1. How awful it is to get rejected.

2. I can't stand this rejection.

3. This rejection makes me an undesirable and unattractive person.

4. I will never have a boyfriend again.

5. Nobody will date me.

Undesirable emotive consequences- Teenager gets depressed, feels anxious, feels worthless.

C- Undesirable behavior consequences. The girl refused to go on another date with someone else as she is afraid of rejection again.

D- Disputing the irrational beliefs

1. Why is it awful to get rejected?
2. Why can't you stand the rejection?
3. How does the rejection make you an undesirable and unattractive person?
4. What makes you think that you will never have a boyfriend again?
5. Where is the evidence that nobody will date you again?

E- Effective disputing or debating irrational beliefs

1. Nothing makes it awful to get rejected. All of us in our lives have experienced rejection one time or another.
2. You can stand the rejection, though you may not like it.
3. Rejection never makes you an undesirable and unattractive person.
4. You can always date others, and eventually will find someone.
5. You are attractive, and eventually someone will ask you for a date again.

The story I narrated actually happened to the daughter of my close family friend. She went through a period of sorrow and self-blaming after her boyfriend broke up with her. Through REBT, she started building confidence in herself, and eventually was dating again and got another boyfriend. She has grown up and is now happily married.

We all have our shares of ups and downs. There is an example of very famous man who failed in business at age 22, ran for legislature and was defeated at age 23, again failed in business at age 34, elected to legislature at age 25, his sweat heart died at age 26, had a nervous breakdown at age 27, defeated for speaker at age 29, defeated for congress at age 34, elected to congress at age 37, defeated for congress at age39, defeated for senate at age 46, defeated for vice president at age 47, defeated for senate at age 49, elected president of the United sates at age 51. The man was Abraham Lincoln. History shows that many intelligent and successful men had their share of setbacks. Albert Einstein was four years old before he could speak. Issac Newton did poorly in grade school and was considered unpromising. Beethoven's music teacher once said to him, "As a composer, he is hopeless. When Thomas Edison was a youngster, his teacher told him he was too stupid to learn anything. Michael Jordan was cut from his high school basketball team. A newspaper editor fired

Walt Disney because he "lacked imagination" and had no good ideas. Winston Churchill failed in the sixth grade.

A person makes mistakes or fails in his attempts, but he is not a failure until he or she gives up and stops trying again. The cognitive distortions or irrational beliefs a person uses and gets stuck in a negative mode are:

1. All or none thinking- A solution is either good or bad, right or wrong; a middle position is not considered.
2. Perfectionistic thinking- Anything less than perfect is unacceptable.
3. Overgeneralization- Broad conclusion driven from little evidence.
4. Catastrophizing- Interpreting events and body sensations as much worse than the available information merits.
5. Self-punishing thinking- Excessive blame of oneself when events happen to a person within.

In REBT, the therapist confronts the patient's cognitive distortions by disputing their irrational belief system and replacing it with rational, pragmatic beliefs to resolve their problems. At times, under stress and difficult circumstances, people get carried away with their belief system (half-jokingly, I call those belief systems B.S.) Especially in circumstances like road rage, when people are getting carried away with their B.S., they don't realize that their beliefs are ironically working against themselves. Cognitive restructuring or reframing involves identifying unrealistic negative thoughts or beliefs and replacing them with more realistic positive ones. Some of us feel overwhelmed under stress, feel helpless and hopeless, and then have tunnel vision. We are not then able to look at the whole picture, and we see half the glass empty rather than half full. In my home, I have a beautiful framed picture of a red rose. Underneath it says," I can complain that red rose bushes have thorns, or rejoice that thornbushes have a rose. It is all up to me".

One of the significant factors that improves the quality of life is a positive attitude. Positive thought processes improve quality of life by injecting a realistic balance into life that appears barren and meaningless, at times. Victor Frankel, a famous psychiatrist, in his book "Man's Search for Meaning "said, "The last thing human freedom-the ability to choose one's attitude in a given set of circumstances".

In my own personal life, I have a series of triumphs and tribulations. It is up to me how I look at my own life. Whenever I feel down, I utilize a positive attitude and optimism, and express gratitude that I have a loving relationship with my life partner. I have two grown-up children and a wonderful grandchild. I have achieved reasonable professional success in my psychotherapy practice. I am financially comfortable in my retirement. I feel fortunate to give financial assistance to many charitable institutions. I have become an author by writing books. I have been able to travel and explore the countries on five continents. Reading, writing, travelling, and service to humanity have been my passions, and I have utilized my potential to achieve the desired goals. It is not only nature and nurture, but our own patience, perseverance, and positive attitude that make the difference in our own judgment and acceptability of our own life. Our satisfaction is related to our own self-efficacy, optimism, positive relationships, and sense of meaning and purpose in life. Fame, fortune, and false pride do not provide real peace and joy. It is the loving kindness, compassion, and meaningful actions that will result in a satisfactory, blissful life. Accept the disappointment and suffering that are inevitable in life. Our personal resources and coping skills are adequate to meet the demands and tasks that confront us.

Carol Ruff (1995) cited six criteria for psychological well-being. They are:

1. Self-acceptance- Ability to acknowledge multiple aspects of self and the ability to accept both positive and negative qualities into a balanced picture of one's abilities.

2. Personal growth- Capacity to grow and develop potential. Personal changes over time that reflect growing self-knowledge and effectiveness, and are open to new experiences.

3. Positive relations with other people- Close, warm, and intimate relationships with others. Concern about the welfare of others, and empathy and affection for other people.

4. Autonomy- Independent and self-determined, the ability to resist social pressure, and the ability to regulate behaviors from within.

5. Purpose of life- A sense of purpose and meaning to life, and a sense of direction and goals in life.

6. Environment mastery- Sense of mastery and competence, and ability to choose situations and environments that are conducive to meeting goals.

Joel Levey and Mischelle Levey (2021), in their book "Living Balance," describe seven key principles of living in balance as attitude, accountability, commitment, supportive relationship, service, personal mastery, and faith.

This author's own experience in life has revealed that good health, self-efficacy/self-esteem, relationship with family and community, conscious purposeful living, emotional balance, and service to humanity contribute significantly to a well-balanced life. Calmness, contentment, and courage are the key ingredients for a peaceful and purposeful life. Count on your inner wisdom to navigate yourself in a rational and pragmatic manner to live a fulfilling and blissful life.

Section 4:
Spiritual Health

Spirituality

Spiritual health and wellness mean a willingness to contemplate some of life's bigger questions: the purpose of your life and how to interpret your deepest values. It also refers to developing respect for nature. It also means connection with your faith and community.

Sadguru, an Indian mystic, stated that true well-being is not only determined by your physical and mental health, but also by the sense of peacefulness, joyfulness, and blissfulness within you. Besides physical and mental health, spirituality is a significant part of life, contributing to living fully, and involves having coherence and congruence among physical, mental, and spiritual aspects of life.

Spirituality is a sacred dimension comprising the deepest values and the meaning by which people live. Spirituality is transcendence, asceticism, and the recognition of one's connection to all. It envisions an inner path enabling persons to discover the essence of their being. Secular spirituality emphasizes humanistic ideas of moral character, qualities such as compassion, patience, tolerance, forgiveness, contentment, responsibility, harmony, and concerns for others. These are aspects of life and human experiences that go beyond the purely material view of the world without necessarily accepting belief in a supernatural reality or divine being.

Spirituality means love, compassion, moral goodness, and self-transcendence. Self-transcendence is the expansion of one's consciousness beyond the self to something higher. According to Victor Frankel, transcendence is rooted in our spirituality and separates us from all other species. One cannot become a fully actualized and whole person without spirituality. Spiritual persons stay ethical and see the world filled with beauty and goodness. Other concepts related to spirituality are consciousness, soul, and enlightenment. Consciousness is the moral sense of right or wrong. Through introspection and evaluation of self, we look into our consciousness. Introspection is a significant part of self-awareness and self-realization. Spiritual persons are aware of the sacred values by which they live. Further, having a calm mind, meditation, and mindfulness also facilitates the consciousness and spiritual process. Consciousness is the energy of the soul. The soul is the spirit and essence of a person (known as atman in Hinduism). Soul is traditionally defined as the spiritual breath of the body. Enlightenment is another concept related to spirituality. An enlightened person uses reason, intellect, and wisdom, involving mental maturity and unbiased thinking.

Comparing/Contrasting Religion vs. Spirituality

Religion and spirituality are two terms that both refer to the beliefs and philosophies of people. They are often used in very similar contexts. There is some overlap between these two terms. An individual's belief in an organized religion may be very spiritual, but spirituality does not always lead the individual to a traditional, organized religious system. Thus, many people describe themselves as spiritual, not religious. Similarly, it is possible to be religious without having a deep spiritual connection with one's faith.

Spirituality is usually associated with an inner search for enlightenment. This may be achieved through practices such as prayer or meditation. It is a very internal process that requires strenuous effort and introspection. Spirituality is often associated with new age beliefs or alternative ideals, but it can also involve an individual's awakening or participation in a conventional religion. The term spirituality usually implies a philosophical or spiritual interest. That is not linked to a particular religion. Spirituality may imply an openness to different interpretations and routes of achieving this connection or understanding, whereas a member of a particular religious group may feel that there is only one true religion.

Religious leaders create doctrine from scriptures interpreted by scholars according to their understanding and vested interest. They preach God's will from a pedestal of authority. They leave no room for the development of the human will to seek and embrace God's will.

One of the biggest differences between religion and spirituality is that religion is based on the past, while spirituality tends to be more about individual development in the present. Religion is based on the teachings of the prophets or spiritual masters like Jesus, Moses, and Buddha, or sayings in holy books like the Gita or the Quran. These teachings are, so to speak, set in stone and cannot be changed, even though the teachings may be outdated, not entirely relevant, and unscientific. Religion is based on myths, folklore stories, mind-boggling miracles, and a traditional established order. On the other hand, in spirituality, an individual can develop their own level of spirituality, which may stem from their own experiences and view of the world. Spirituality does not require participating in rituals or following religious laws. Spirituality tends to be much more the individual sort of connection with a higher power in their own unique way. Spirituality is more about an inner quest rather than an outward performance. Spirituality is about finding one's own path, which requires the assistance of religious leaders, but which can also be achieved alone or through conventional means.

Religion is based on blind faith, customs, and traditions of old times. Science evolved, new awareness emerged, but the rules and regulations and holy books never changed. So, organized religions always remained within confined boundaries. Shawn Paul, in his book on "Religions, Spirituality and Humanity," states that it is not the true doctrines of religions, but the customs and traditions that, at times, create mass hysteria and cause unrest and agitation in the public. As sin distorts our moral judgment, clouds our thinking, and hinders our fellowship with others, blind faith and extremism can distort moral judgment, cloud our thinking, and hinder our fellowship with others.

True religion is based on compassion, peace, and love. Religion that recognizes human life, human dignity, and justice for all, regardless of their particular faith. True religion consists of moral excellence, living a life of purity, altruism, hear no evil, see no evil, and do no evil. Reciting holy books does not make a person holy. Man should have full conviction in the true Divine law and, most importantly, experience, practice, and follow the moral code of life. The moral code of good conduct consists of purity of mind, devotion, humility, and charity.

Purity is the pristine and natural state of the soul. Cultivate purity by maintaining a clean and healthy body, keeping good company, and leading a disciplined life.

Devotion is love of God or goodness. It involves dedication to family and friends. Being loyal, trustworthy, and selfless in service.

Humility is a mildness, modesty, reverence, and unpretentiousness. Cultivate humility by showing patience with circumstances and forbearance with people.

Charity is a selfless concern and caring for our fellow men. Giving to the hungry, homeless, sick, the elderly, and the destitute. Good conduct is a combination of avoiding unethical behaviors and performing virtues, spiritualizing acts.

The true purpose of the religion is based on truthfulness, honesty, and love for the right. True aspects of all religions call for compassion, austerity, cooling of passion, inner and outer purity, control of senses, self-restraint, service to humanity, and equality among all living beings. These aspects of true doctrines of religions incline persons to become spiritual persons of moral character, having patience, compassion, and concern for others. Thus, the true nature and positive features of religions are interconnected with spirituality.

Traditional Spirituality

Abrahamic Faiths:

Judaism: The musar movement is a Jewish spiritual movement that has focused on developing character traits such as faith, humility, and love. It encouraged spiritual practices of Jewish meditation, Jewish prayer, Jewish ethics, and the study of Musar(ethical) literature.

Christianity- Catholic spirituality is the spiritual practice of living out a personal act of faith following the acceptance of faith. Although all Catholics are expected to pray together at Mass, there are many different forms of spirituality and private prayer that have developed over the centuries. Progressive Christianity is a contemporary movement that seeks to remove the supernatural claims of faith and replace them with a post-critical understanding of biblical spirituality based on historical and scientific research. It focuses on the lived experience of spirituality over historical dogmatic claims, and accepts that faith is both true and a human construction and that spiritual experiences are psychologically and mentally real and useful.

Islam- The pillars of Islam are five basic acts in Islam considered obligatory for all believers. The Quran presents them as a framework for worship and a sign of commitment to the faith. They are 1. The creed 2. Daily prayers 3. Alms giving 4. Fasting during Ramadan, and 5. The pilgrimage to Mecca is once in a lifetime. Sufis consider themselves the original true proponents of the pure form of Islam. They are strong adherents to the principles of tolerance and peace and are against any form of violence. The Darquana Sufi teacher Ahmed Ibn Ajiba described Sufiism as a science through which we can know how to travel into the presence of the Divine, purify oneself from filth, and beautify with a variety of praiseworthy acts.

Hinduism- Traditionally, Hinduism identifies three ways of spiritual practice, namely jnana. The way of knowledge, bhakti, the way of devotion, and *Karma* yoga, the way of selfless action. In the nineteenth century, Vivekananda, in his Neo-Vedanta synthesis of Hinduism, and Raja Yoga, the way of contemplation and meditation, as a fourth way, called all of them yoga. The Jnana path is often assisted by a guru(teacher) in one's spiritual practice. The bhakti path is devotion to deity or deities. The spiritual practice often includes chanting, singing, such as kirtan (group singing of religious nature), in front of idols or images of one or more, or a devotional symbol of the holy. The karma way is the path of one's work, especially diligence, honesty, and hard work toward fulfillment of one's effort for the desired goal, not necessarily for material rewards. The Raja Yoga path is one of cultivating necessary virtues, self-discipline, meditation, contemplation, and self-reflection to a pinnacle state called samadhi. The state of samadhi (meditative practice) refers to the development of a luminous mind that is equanimous and mindful. The state of samadhi has been compared to peak experience. Personally, this author likes to change bhakti path as a devotion to the deeper inner values of patience, love, and purity of mind. This will thus fulfill the spiritual quest for the individual.

Modern spirituality is centered on deeper values and the meaning by which a person lives. It envisions an inner path enabling a person to discover the essence of his/her being. Contemporary spirituality theorists assert that spirituality develops inner peace and forms a foundation for happiness. Inspirations, aspirations, and realization are rungs of the spiritual ladder. Spirituality leads to bliss and inner contentment. Spiritual practices include fasting, self-discipline, patience, concerns for others, meditation, and cultivating calmness, as well as social practices like selfless charitable work. Spirituality involves love, the value of thoughtfulness, and ethical work aimed towards the betterment of all. Scientific research shows a positive correlation between spirituality and mental well-being, higher intrinsic meaning in life, and inner peace. There is growing interest in spiritual care within the health profession to improve the outcome of medical treatment.

Yoga and spiritual health- First two limbs of yoga, Yamas (restraints, mental discipline or control) and *Niyamas*(observance) are directly linked to moral codes and spiritual practices. The Yamas or restraints are divided into five moral injunctions aimed at destroying the lower nature.

They should be practiced and developed not only by the letter but also, more importantly, in the spirit. These five moral disciplines are:

Ahimsa or non-violence

Ahimisa Satya, or truthfulness

Brahmacharya or moderation in all things (control of senses). Also refers to celibacy.

Asteya or non-stealing

Aparigraha-or non-covetousness

Practice Yamas by being kind and honest, and how you speak to yourself and others

Niyamas or Observances (DO's) are also divided into five ethical percepts.

They are:

Saucha or purity- Internal and external purity, cleanliness

Santosha or contentment

Tapas or austerity, discipline

Svadhyaya, or the study of sacred texts and the self

Ishwara Pranidhana, who is constantly living with an awareness of the Divine presence.

You can practice *Niyamas* by keeping your space and body clean. Eat well and practice gratitude. Niyamas, or positive duties or observances, are thought of as recommended habits for a healthy living and spiritual existence. Yamas and Niyamas together are significant aspects of spiritual wellness.

Cultivating Spirituality

Cultivating a deeper spirituality means getting in touch with your inner self as well as embodying love, expressed as gratitude, compassion, acceptance, forgiveness, hope and unselfishness. Mayo Clinic guide to Holistic Health has delineated ways to cultivate spirituality through the following: prayers, meditation, mindfulness, reading inspirational stories, and finding purpose and meaning in life.

Purpose and Meaning of Life

Spiritual love can refer to love rooted in spiritual connection that helps us find meaning and purpose in life. The purpose of life is to find out who you really are, to grow and evolve, to reach a higher state of consciousness, to experience the Divine, and to become enlightened. Meaning refers to how we make sense of life and our roles in it.

Having a meaningful life can be facilitated by greater awareness of core values and the thoughts behind them. The insight provided by understanding positive values can help regain a sense of meaning to improve motivation. Victor Frankel's meaning of life can be discussed in three ways.

1. By creating work or accomplishing some task.
2. By experiencing something fully or loving someone.
3. By the attitude that we adopt toward unavoidable suffering.

The meaning and purpose of life is based on truthfulness, honesty, and love for the right. The purpose of life is to have greater harmony, coherence, and congruence among the various aspects of self, service to others, dedication to a worthy cause, live life fully and deeply as possible, and spiritual experience. Positive goals and striving for achievement increase alignment with your values. Values represent what we consider essential and what we love in life. You can find purpose and meaning in life by

1. Identifying the things that you care about.
2. Reflecting on what matters most.
3. Recognizing your strengths and talents.
4. Improving your best possible self.
5. Cultivating positive emotions.
6. Look to people you admire.

Developing purpose is a personal journey and must come from within. It emerges from contemplation and higher-order goals, and answers questions like, Why am I here? What matters most? How can I make the world a better place?

Reflection can help cultivate your sense of purpose.

1. Reflect on what you value and how you want to show up in the world. What is most meaningful?
2. Consider your life role- Identify those that are most important to you. Prioritize your role and responsibility by articulating why they are important to you and how they might relate.
3. Reflect on what gives you a sense of deep satisfaction or joy. Are there certain things you are especially good at and enjoy doing?
4. Identify positive goals in life, like service to others and dedication to a worthy cause.
5. Reflection to strengthen your sense of purpose.

In the Hindu Vedic scriptures, the aims of human life are indicated by *Dharma, Artha, Kama,* and *Moksha*. These are known as *Purusharthas* (objectives of human life).

Dharma (righteousness, ethics)- Dharma is considered the foremost goal of a human being. It includes duties, rights, laws, conduct, virtues, and the right way of living. Dharma includes religious duties, moral rights, and duties of each individual, as well as behavior that enables social order, right conduct, and virtues.

Artha (livelihood, wealth)- Artha is the objective and virtuous pursuit of wealth for livelihood, obligations, and economic prosperity. The proper pursuit of Artha is considered an important aim of human life in Hinduism.

Kama (sensual, pleasure)- Kama means desire, wish, passion, longing, pleasure of senses, the aesthetic enjoyment of life, affection, or love, with or without sexual connotations. Kama is considered an essential and healthy goal of human life when pursued without sacrificing dharma.

Moksha (liberation, freedom)- Moksha is a concept associated with liberation from sorrow, suffering and samsara (the birth and rebirth cycle) in and after life, particularly in the theistic school of Hinduism. In another school of Hinduism, such as monistic theism, moksha is a goal achievable in current life, as a stable state of bliss and self-realization, comprehending the nature of one's soul, of freedom, and of realizing the whole universe as the self.

The purpose of life in Hinduism consists of these four objectives. Another concept in this context is *SAT Chit Anand. Sat means truth, chit means awareness or consciousness*, and Anand means bliss. Thus, Sat, Chit, and Anand evolve the bliss of pure knowledge and consciousness. This is realized through direct self-realization. Sat, Chit, Anand is a spiritual concept related to awareness of our consciousness, truth, reality, and blissfulness in our life.

Having a strong sense of purpose in life is linked to higher levels of well-being, happiness, and resilience. Those who have a higher sense of purpose take better care of themselves, function better, experience fewer chronic conditions, have better mental health, and live longer.

Famous quotes concerning spirituality are:

Treat not others in ways that you yourself would find hurtful-------------------Buddha

Do not do to others what you do not want done to yourself----------------- Confucius

Do not do to others what would cause pain if done to you----------   Mahabharata

In everything do to others as you would do to you, for this is the law---   Jesus

Do not do unto others, whatever is injurious to yourself--------------------Zoroaster

What is hateful to you, do not do to your neighbor. This is the whole Torah, the rest is commentary-

Rabbi Hillel--The Talmud

Not one of them truly believes until they wish for others what you wish for yourself-Muhammad

All the religions and ancient spiritual masters have stated the same thing: that we need to have compassion, empathy, and concern for our brethren. If we follow this simple spiritual advice, promote the concept of syncretism to create harmony between different faiths, and develop common bonds to promote peace, then we will have spiritual blissfulness.

Section 5:
Global Health /Wellness

Global health is an area for study, research, and practice that places a priority on improving health and achieving equity in health for all. Wellness is an active pursuit of activities, choices, and lifestyles that lead to a state of holistic health.

Everyone should have the opportunity to live a life that supports good health. However, vast differences in people's environments, resources, and social status affect the choices available to them. Achieving equity in health means addressing social and environmental determinants and eliminating disparities in the health system and health care access.

Global disparity

Rainn Wilson, in his book Soul Boom, states that there are unjust economic extremes. The world's eight richest men currently own as much wealth as the poorest 50 percent of the world population. The top three billionaires own financial assets as much as the poorest forty-eight countries combined. The grotesque wealth disparity affects health care, education, nutrition, food scarcity, child mortality, and countless other issues that devastate the world's poor.

Oxfam reports that from March 18 to the end of 2020, Global billionaires' wealth increased by 3.9 trillion. By contrast, global workers' combined earnings fell by 3.7 trillion. According to the Credit Suisse Health report, in 2021, the world's richest 1 percent, those with more than $1 million, own 47.8% of all the world's wealth. Adults with less than $10,000 in wealth make 53.2 percent of the world population, but hold just 1,1 percent of global wealth. Individuals owning over $100,000 in assets make up 13 percent of the global population, but own 85.6 percent of global wealth. The richest 1 percent captured 54 percent of new global wealth over the past decade. This has accelerated to 63 percent in the past ten years. Forty-two trillion dollars of new wealth was created between December 2019 and December 2021. Twenty-six trillion (63 percent) went to the richest 1 percent while 16 trillion (37 percent) went to the bottom 99 percent. Oxfam research also shows that the ultra-rich are the biggest industrial contributors to the climate crisis. The richest billionaires, through their pollution investment, are emitting a million times more carbon than the average person. The wealthiest 1 percent of humanity are responsible for twice as many emissions as the poorest 50 percent.

Rainn Wilson remarks on how much effort, research, and technology we put into creating missiles, guns, warships, bombs, nuclear subs, fighter jets, and other countless horrific weapons of mass destruction. What if humanity spent the same amount of time, money, and energy working on healing and caring for diseases like cancer and other diseases and taking care of climate change?

Rainn Wilson, in his book Soul Boom, commented that we need to shift our view of true success away from the accumulation of wealth and towards nobility, selflessness, and generosity. U.S. and other Western countries continue to have material wealth while ignoring the human needs of the rest of the planet. This author strongly believes that we need to pay more attention to gross national contentment (GNC) rather than gross national product (GNP).

Vipin Mehta, in his book Global Healing, New Vista of Hope, states that in order to change the world, we have to change the mindset. Extreme nationalism and dogmatic ideas are luxuries that the human race can no longer afford. Through generosity, compassion, love, and caring, we create oneness among members of the global family. It is in this state that we are able to see the true nature of reality, to see our purpose, and to have clarity in regard to our interdependence.

Global health statistics indicate that the top ten causes of death account for 55.4 million deaths worldwide. Three broader categories are cardiovascular (ischemic heart disease, strokes), respiratory (chronic obstructive pulmonary disease (COPD), and neonatal conditions, which include birth asphyxia and birth trauma, neonatal sepsis and infection, and preterm birth complications. Noncommunicable diseases together accounted for 74% deaths globally in 2019. The world's biggest health killer is ischemic heart disease, responsible for 16% of the world's total deaths. Since 2000, the largest increase in deaths has been for this disease, rising from more than 2 million to 8.9 million deaths in 2019. Strokes and COPD are the second and third leading causes of death, responsible for approximately 11 % and 6% of total deaths. Lower respiratory infection remains the world's leading communicable disease, ranked as the fourth leading cause of death. The number of deaths has gone down substantially, in 2019 at 2.6 million, 460,000 fewer than in 2000. Measuring how people die helps to assess the effectiveness of our death system and direct resources to where they are needed most. The World Health Organization (WHO) develops standards and best practices for data collection, processing, and synthesizing through the consolidated and improved International Classification of Diseases (ICD-11).

A lack of medical, water, and electricity; shortage of doctors; prohibitive costs: they all stand in the way of providing good quality health care to all. The WHO report states that half of the world lacks access to essential health services, and 100 million people are still pushed into extreme poverty because of health expenses. It is extremely unacceptable that half of the world still lacks coverage for the most essential health services. There is some good news: The reports show that the 21st century has seen an increase in the number of people able to obtain some key health services, such as immunization and family planning, as well as antiretroviral treatment for HIV, and insecticide-treated bed nets to prevent malaria. Fewer people are now tipped into extreme poverty than at the turn of the century. Progress, however, is very uneven. There are wide gaps in the availability of services in Sub-Saharan Africa and other southern Asia. Without health care, how can children reach their full potential? And without a healthy, productive population, how can societies realize their aspirations? Every year, nearly six million die in developing countries from low-quality health care.

Strategies for improving health care in developing countries include;

1. Long-term economic growth
2. Biomedical intervention
3. Improving water sources and sanitation
4. Better diets
5. Improving women's rights and maternal health
6. Providing cheaper drugs
7. Controlling corporations.

This author's main concern is poverty in poor countries, contributing to hunger, malnutrition, and lack of basic needs of food, shelter, and clothing, and further difficulties in accessing primary education and basic health care. Hunger is a serious problem among poverty-stricken children in poor countries. Every day, more than 10,000 children die from hunger-related causes. Malnutrition affects children throughout their lives. It causes a deficiency in their physical and mental growth and impairs their ability to learn. Political instability, food and agriculture policies, and climate change are some of the factors responsible for food shortages. The combined efforts of international aid organizations can help increase food supply and avoid waste. Such efforts have resulted in reducing hunger throughout the world.

In a world grappling with food shortages in poor countries, one often overlooked contribution to the situation is food waste. Every year, a staggering amount of food ends up in landfills, emitting greenhouse gases and exacerbating the global climate crisis. According to Feeding America, the U.S. misuses 119 billion pounds of food annually, equivalent to 130 billion meals and a staggering $408 billion in discarded food. Nearly 40% of all food in America is wasted. What's even more alarming is that this figure is estimated to increase by 21% to 25% between Thanksgiving and the New Year.

Another big problem is that America consumes too much meat. Americans are the world champions of meat eaters. Each American, on average, consumes 327 pounds of meat annually, tying the country for first in meat consumption. Studies indicate that merely cutting meat consumption in half, Americans eat as much animal flesh as the Danes. And going from the equivalent of a daily quarter-pounder to one every other day would slash diet-related carbon emissions by 43%. It could also reduce the incidence of obesity, cancer, and other illnesses.

Consider these statistics about the global animal agriculture industry:

Livestock cover 45% of the Earth's total land area.

Global greenhouse gas emission- 51% due to livestock and byproducts; 13% due to transportation (road, rail, air & marine).

A plant-based diet cuts your carbon footprint by 50%.

Livestock is 65% nitrous oxide, responsible for emissions.

Deforestation- 1-2 acres of rainforest are cleared every second.

Animal agriculture is responsible for 91% of Amazon destruction

Water use: 1 hamburger = 600 gallons of water, equivalent to showering for 2 months. The meat & dairy industry uses 1/3 of Earth's fresh water.

U.S. Water use- 5% domestic, 55% animal agriculture

Land use- 1/3 land decertified due to livestock. Livestock covers 45% of the Earth's total land

1.5 acres of land = 37000 lbs. of plant food or 375 lbs. of meat.

Plant-based food is much more sustainable and has a significantly lower carbon footprint by using less overall land, water, and other resources. Adopting a vegan diet would lessen the need for as much livestock and free up more natural resources and food grown to be available directly as food to feed more people instead of animals. An increase in the supply of plant-based products would also be available to directly tackle world hunger, help address climate change, and create a more efficient food production to feed the world's growing population.

More prosperous nations tend to have more adequate food supply, better drinking water, better schools, better human rights, and more income equity, as well as a number of other indicators of a higher quality of life. There needs to be a balance between individual and collective well-being. We do not live in isolation. We are all part of the planet Earth. Bjorn Lomberg, in his book "Best Things First," has outlined 12 efficient solutions for the poor half of the world. Based on peer review research, Lomberg has identified 12 of the most efficient policies that dramatically improve the lives of people living in the poorer half of the world. For about $35 billion per year, we can save 4.2 million lives annually, and we make the poor half of the world more than a trillion dollars better off each and every year. The author claims that we can almost entirely end tuberculosis, which needlessly kills more than a million people each year. We can reduce the death toll of chronic diseases by 1.5 million. We can increase yield in agriculture, make farmers produce more while avoiding hunger for more than a hundred million people. Investment of $35 billion is a tiny fraction of the trillions of dollars we spend on military and weapons of mass destruction. In the 20th century, human relations and the sustainability of the plant have taken a secondary place compared to advances in science and technology. As a result, the disparity between the rich and the poor has been widened.

To address the inequality and further improve health conditions in poor countries, it includes combating hunger, access to clean drinking water, and sanitation. Shawn Paul, in his book Religions, Spirituality, and Humanity, describes the humanitarian projects providing the material and logistical assistance to a group of people or to a country in need of aid. Humanitarian projects focus on poverty-stricken areas. These areas have been in poverty for a long time, and living conditions and quality of life are far below the adequate living standard. Humanitarian projects to these parts of the world usually send aid such as money, farming tools, medicine, and building materials. Humanitarian organizations like the World Food Program, Oxfam, and the Red Cross have been at the forefront of combating child hunger problems. Current humanitarian projects include reducing poverty, coordinating international humanitarians to provide emergency help in case of natural and man-made disasters, and providing humanitarian aid to boost the economy. Global Wellness Institute (GWI) empowers the wellness world worldwide by educating the public and private sectors about preventable diseases. The GWI serves as a "hub: that informs and connects key stakeholders capable of impacting the overall well-being of our planet's citizens. Some of these initiatives' projects include nutrition for healing, a healthy baby guide, access to clean drinking water, mental wellness, and workplace well-being. GWI is a valuable source of guidance and assistance to the poverty-stricken population.

Transcending to global well-being

I envision a day when all nations, as a global family, will join hands together towards building an egalitarian society where all beings cooperate for the common good of all citizens of the world, where the inherent and intrinsic worth of all humans is recognized, where all beings have an opportunity to lead a meaningful and purposeful life, where there is a global peace established through mutual compassion and concern for all living beings. Where there is a regard for our precious environment and concern for human ecology. Where human resources are utilized wisely and efficiently. Where every human has an opportunity to grow and evolve to his or her full potential. Where, irrespective of caste, creed, or color, everybody is treated equally. I envision a society inclusive of all nations, all races, religions, and genders integrated into a harmonious, peaceful, and prosperous global family. In this way, we embark on an ambitious journey of humanity, comprising social justice and peaceful coexistence, and a nature-loving noble global family. I complete this section with a Vedic Sanskrit quote along with translation as follows;

Sarvesam Svaster Bhantu (May there be well-being in all);

Sarvesam Shantir Bhantu (May there be peace in all);

Sarvesam Purnam Bhantu (May there be completeness in all);

Sarvesam Manglam Bhantu (May there be success in all).

OM Shanti Shanti Shanti (Chanting peace in body, mind, and spirit)

Section 6:
Summary and Conclusions

Harmony and balance in living exist when there is an integrated focus on all essential aspects of life. Buddha teaches us that freedom and happiness will not be found in the extreme of either sensual indulgence or spiritual purification; a middle way is essential. It is the noble path that transcends these two extremes and leads to enlightenment, wisdom, and peace of mind. There is a need to have a balance between freedom and responsibility; otherwise, there will be chaos in society. Balance is necessary between work and home life. Life will be full of peace, love, and joy if there is harmony between the physical, mental, emotional, and spiritual aspects of life.

The physical body is the foundation of healthy well-being. "Mens sana in corpore sono" is a classical Latin phrase which means A healthy mind in a healthy body." Further, if our limbic system (emotional mind) is aligned with the conscious mind (mental health), then there is a harmony between emotions and the conscious mind. When the mind is aligned with the spiritual realm, then blissfulness is achieved. Thus, harmony and balance between the healthy body, mind, and spirit will result in our holistic well-being. Righteous living is living consciously every moment with intentions and awareness. We are responsible for our thoughts, feelings, and actions individually and collectively. There needs to be a balance between nature, community, and human spirits. We need to be mindful of our responsibility to ourselves, our family, community, and nation, and be compassionate and caring to our brethren throughout the world.

Physical dimension has to do with the body, its function, and activities that support it; our mental dimension includes thoughts and attitudes. The emotional realm is connected with feelings. Finally, the spiritual dimension is equally important as it refers to what an individual holds sacred in their life. The spiritual aspects also include leading a noble life of honesty, empathy, compassion, and loving kindness. It is essential that these significant aspects of life be integrated with each other to have a harmonious and balanced life.

Balanced diet, regular exercise, and sufficient sleep work together to keep your body healthy. An optimum diet is a significant part of physical health as it provides nutrition, vitamins, minerals,

119

and energy. Seven essential elements for a balanced diet include carbohydrates, protein, fat, fiber, vitamins, minerals, and water. Carbohydrates, protein, and fat are three micronutrients in your diet. According to the WHO, 80 percent of heart disease, stroke, and type 2 diabetes, and 40 percent of cancer could be prevented with improvements to diet and lifestyle. A healthy diet is a calorie-controlled, plant-based diet with less meat, sugar, and salt and more protein. This means eating a lot of vegetables, fruit, and nuts, choosing whole grain foods, limiting processed food, and restricting or even avoiding red meat altogether. Keep your body well hydrated all the time. Clean water is the best drink.

Physical activity, such as a balanced diet, helps improve overall health and quality of life. Physical activity keeps your heart and circulatory system healthy and provides protection against numerous chronic diseases. It can also strengthen muscles, which can reduce older people's risk of falls. If we spend adult years building up our muscle mass, our strength, our balance, our cardiovascular endurance, then as the body ages, we are starting from a stronger place. The best exercise is any activity you enjoy doing and will stick with. The American Heart Association recommends 150 minutes of moderate-intensity exercise per week. Walking for a little more than 20 minutes is beneficial. Benefits of regular physical activities include weight management, lowering risk for cardiovascular disease, reducing risk of developing type 2 diabetes, helping reduce risk of infectious diseases, lowering risk for developing several kinds of cancer, strengthening your bones and muscles, improving daily activities, increasing your chances of living longer, and managing chronic health conditions.

Like eating nutritious food and exercising, getting quality sleep is an important component of your overall health. Quality sleep is associated with a balanced life. Most adults should get between seven and nine hours of sleep each night. While sleeping, the body performs a number of repairing and maintenance processes that affect nearly every part of the body. During sleep, the body rests, cleans and purifies itself, rebuilds, grows, and heals itself. Health benefits of sleep include improved mood, a healthy heart, regulation of blood sugar, improved mental function, restoring the immune system, and stress relief and maintaining a healthy weight.

To avoid health complications and maintain good health, it is important to know certain parameters about ideal health. What is considered a normal range of values? BMI or body mass index: normal< 25, overweight 25-29, obese 30 or higher, morbid obesity>40. Overweight and obesity contribute to many diseases, and hence you must try to keep your BMI below 25.

Blood Pressure (B.P.): Normal 120/80 or below; Stage 1 hypertension 130-139/ 80-89; Stage 2 hypertension 140-179 /90 and up; hypertension crisis. 180 and up/120 and up. 180/120 is a sharp increase in B.P., which may cause stroke.

Lipid (Cholesterol) Profile: Normal cholesterol <200 mg/dl. LDL (low density lipoprotein) or bad cholesterol -100mg/dl or less. HDL (high-density lipoprotein) or good cholesterol is desirable at 60 mg/dl. Excess cholesterol, especially high LDL, contributes to vascular atherosclerosis.

Fasting blood sugar (FBS) and HBA1C: Normal FBS is 100mg/dl or below. Pre-diabetes 100-125. Diabetes >125. Your post-prandial blood sugar should be <180, ideally <150. HbA1C non diabetic range is below 5.7. Pre-diabetic 5.7-6.4, and above 6.5 is consistent with diabetes.

To prevent serious health problems like heart disease, cancer, stroke, diabetes, and improve overall health, include quitting smoking, controlling blood pressure, maintaining a healthy weight, eating a low-fat, low-salt diet that is rich in fruits and vegetables, whole grains, regular exercise, and adequate sleep.

Physical health and mental health are intertwined. Your brain is a part of your body, and your body communicates with your brain to help you function. It is important to know that emotions and mental health are interlinked. Emotional well-being can help people manage their mental disorders better, as well as provide an outlet for dealing with stress and psychological issues. On the other hand, good emotional well-being can be disrupted if there is an underlying issue with our mental health. Characteristics of an emotionally healthy person are that they are self-aware, perceive themselves accurately, and understand how their behavior comes across to others. They have emotional agility and are able to adapt, align, and perform well. Further, they have strong and healthy coping skills, live with purpose, and manage stress well. Taking active steps towards emotional and mental health can lead to improved emotional regulation, better self-esteem and confidence, increased motivation and productivity, and a heightened sense of overall well-being. Activities that help improve emotional/mental health include expressing feelings, talking about worries and concerns with friends and family. Develop positive coping skills such as mindfulness, meditation, or exercise, practicing self-care like getting enough rest, eating well, and engaging in activities like hobbies or sports, and seeking support from a mental health professional if necessary. Taking a holistic approach to overall well-being.

Pertinent issues to improve mental/ emotional well-being are: stress, anxiety, and anger management, effective communications and social skills, work-life balance, developing intimacy, fulfillment of innate needs, and achieving happiness. The three Cs of stress management are commitment, control, and challenge. Commitment means personal commitment to work and personal life, control means you can influence events in your life, and challenge means you view demands as challenging rather than a threat. Change is an opportunity, and challenges are positive and invigorating. Other ways to manage stress include relaxation techniques such as deep breathing, body scan, progressive muscle relaxation, biofeedback, meditation, guided imagery, cognitive reappraisal, social support system, and adequate sleep. These methods are equally beneficial to relieve and manage anxiety. Meditation and mindfulness have sweeping health benefits, such as developing self-control and bringing the mind and body into focus.

Having supportive family and friends results in enhanced mental health, a sense of belongingness, and better self-esteem. Effective communication and social skills improve confidence, build better positive relationships with colleagues, and within the family. A healthy work-life balance refers to maintaining a harmonious relationship between your work and personal life. It involves consciously managing your time and energy to meet both professional and personal commitments while prioritizing self-care and well-being. Find work that makes you yearn for balance and that provides moments of satisfaction, accomplishments, and connection. The quality of our relationship is one of the central factors in whether we feel content, satisfied, and happy with our lives. Intimacy and love are significant parts of enhancing our relationships with loved ones. One of the main foundations of a healthy relationship is the ability to trust one another. Trust, sincerity, mutual understanding, companionship, friendship, respect, similarity in attitude and values, reciprocity, mutual exchange of positive emotions, self-disclosure, warmth, dependability, and emotional stability contribute to intimacy. Sternberg's triangular theory of love holds that consummate or complete love involves components of passion, intimacy, and commitment. Love is one of the most important components of a fulfilling life. Before we love someone, we need to love ourselves, accept ourselves as we are, and then move on to love someone else.

Peace is possible when you have good health and basic needs of food, shelter, and clothing, including a safe environment to live. When you have a sense of belonging, and you have a loving family, friends, and community. These are the basic hierarchy of needs. When you feel good about yourself, have self-worth, and you transcend to self-actualization, then you have joy or bliss. In general, in Western society, most people have their basic needs of physiological, safety, security, and belongingness met to a significant degree. Problems start with esteem needs. Many people do not feel good about themselves. These contribute to problems of depression, anxiety, relationships, work, and overall mental/emotional well-being. Steps to build self-esteem include taking responsibility for your decisions, developing expertise in some area, setting goals, thinking positively about yourself, learn new skills, taking pride in your achievements, paying attention to your thoughts and feelings, exploring and appreciating your talents, and loving yourself.

True happiness is centered on finding positive emotions in life, meaning often involves recognizing and accepting both positive and negative emotions, accepting and integrating all emotions, and having a profound connection with others. The core variables that both predict happiness and satisfaction in life in Western individualized culture are: positive self-esteem, sense of perceived control, extroversion, optimism, positive social relationships, and sense of meaning and purpose in life. Eudaimonia is a state or condition of "good spirit" and what is commonly translated as "happiness". Eudaimonia is a much deeper and richer concept than happiness. It is more stable and cannot be quickly taken from us. The stoic happiness triangle demonstrates that the ideal human state of existence was where one's wisdom, living with virtues, self-control, and personal responsibility, blended together. This condition is eudaimonia. Eudaimonia in Vedic is equated with bliss, which is equal to supreme happiness, utter joy, or contentment. Authentic happiness is living in peace and harmony with your body, mind, and soul. Happy people pursue intrinsic goals, enjoy the moment, have balance, a realistic view of events, cultivate strong relationships, and show gratitude.

There are many types of therapeutic interventions to help individuals with their struggles and overcome difficult circumstances. One of the extremely effective therapeutic approaches is Cognitive Restructuring. This technique comes from Cognitive Behavior Therapy (CBT). Another version of CBT is Rational Emotive Behavior Therapy (REBT). It is based on the first-century A.D. philosopher Epictetus, who said, "men are disturbed not by the things but the view which they take of them". Psychologist Alert Ellis stated that it is not the events that directly cause emotions and behaviors. Rather, it is one's belief about the events that lead to emotional and behavioral reactivity. Having Cognitive distortions or irrational beliefs can contribute to negative consequences. By disputing the irrational beliefs and replacing them with rational, pragmatic beliefs, we can resolve the problematic issues. At times, under stress and difficult circumstances, people get carried away with their own belief system, like in road rage cases, not realizing their beliefs are ironically working against them. Some of us feel overwhelmed under stress, feel helpless and hopeless, and then have tunnel vision. We have not been able to look at the whole picture and see it as half glass empty rather than half full. One of the significant factors that improves quality of life is a positive attitude. Positive thought process improves quality of life by injecting a realistic balance into life that appears barren and meaningless at times. Victor Frankel, in his book "Man's Search for Meaning," said the last thing human freedom is -the ability to choose one's attitude in a given set of circumstances. In my own personal life, I utilize a positive attitude and optimism and express gratitude for all the good things that have happened in my life. It is not only nature and nurture, but our own patience, perseverance, and positive attitude that make the difference. Positive satisfaction in life depends upon our own judgment and the acceptability of our own life. Fame, fortune, and false pride do not provide real peace and joy. It is the loving kindness, compassion, and meaningfulness that will result in a satisfactory, blissful life. Accept the disappointment and suffering that are inevitable in life. Our personal resources and coping skills are adequate to meet the demands and tasks that confront us.

Joel Levey and Michelle Levey, in their book Living Balance, describe seven key principles of balanced living as attitude, accountability, commitment, supportive relationship, service, personal mastery, and faith. This author's experiences of counseling others and his own life have made him realize that the key to a well-balanced life is based on good health, self-efficacy/ self-esteem, relationship with family and community, conscious purposeful living, emotional balance, and service to humanity. Count on your inner wisdom to navigate yourself in a rational and pragmatic manner to live a fulfilling, blissful life.

Spirituality is a significant part of life, contributing to living fully, and involves having coherence and congruence among physical, emotional, and spiritual aspects of life. Spirituality is a sacred dimension comprising the deepest values and the meaning by which people live. It envisions an inner path enabling a person to discover the essence of their being. Secular spirituality emphasizes a humanistic idea of moral character, qualities such as compassion, patience, tolerance, forgiveness, contentment, responsibility, harmony, and concerns for others. Spirituality is a part of humanity that separates us from all other species. One cannot become a fully actualized and whole person without spirituality. Spiritual people stay ethical and see the world filled with beauty and goodness.

Religion and spirituality are two terms that both refer to the beliefs and philosophies of people. They are often used in very similar contexts. An individual's belief in an organized religion may be very spiritual, but spirituality does not always lead the individual to a traditional, organized religious system. Thus, many people describe themselves as spiritual, not religious. Spirituality is usually associated with an inner search for enlightenment. This may be achieved through practices such as prayers or meditation. One of the biggest differences between religion and spirituality is that religion is based on the past, while spirituality tends to be more about individual development in the present. Religion is based on the teachings of the prophets or spiritual masters like Jesus, Moses, and Buddha, or sayings in a holy book like the Gita or the Quran. Religion is based on established order, customs, and traditions of old times. On the other hand, spiritual individuals can develop their own level of spirituality, which may stem from their experience and view of their world.

True doctrines of the religion are based on truthfulness, honesty, compassion, austerity, cooling of passion, inner and outer purity, control of senses, self-restraint, service to humanity, and equality among all living beings. These aspects of true doctrines of religion incline a person to become a spiritual person of moral character, having patience, compassion, and concern for others. Thus, the true doctrines and positive features of religions are interconnected and intertwined with spirituality.

Spirituality develops inner peace and forms a foundation of true happiness. Spirituality leads to bliss and inner contentment. Spirituality practices include fasting, self-discipline, patience, meditation, and cultivating calmness, as well as social practices like selflessness and charitable work. Spirituality involves love, thoughtfulness, and ethical work aimed towards the betterment of all. Scientific research shows a positive correlation between spirituality and mental health and well-being, higher intrinsic meaning in life, and inner peace.

Spiritual love can refer to love rooted in a spiritual connection that helps us find meaning and purpose in our lives. The purpose of life is to find out who you really are, to grow and evolve, to reach a higher state of consciousness, to experience the divine, and to become enlightened. Meaning refers to how we make sense of life and our roles in it. The meaning and purpose of life is based on truthfulness, honesty, and love for the right. The purpose of life is to have greater harmony and coherence, and congruence among various aspects of self, service to others, dedication to a worthy cause, live life fully and deeply as possible, and spiritual experience. Positive goals and striving for achievement increase alignment with your values. Having a strong sense of purpose in life is linked to a higher level of well-being, happiness, and resilience. Those who have a higher sense of purpose take care of themselves, function better, experience fewer chronic conditions, have better mental health, and live longer.

Yoga is often seen as a spiritual practice that promotes the connection between body, mind, and spirit. Yoga is a physical, mental, and spiritual discipline that aids in relaxation, emotional regulation, flexibility, strength, balance, and concentration. Yoga has been proven to be beneficial in the treatment of stress, anxiety, depression, and mood disorders as it creates a greater sense of well-being. The posture of yoga is designed to strengthen your body from the inside to the outside. Mental endurance and physical stamina are tested by holding a posture for a certain amount of time. In the meditative practice of yoga, we direct our awareness inwards and learn to identify negative thought patterns and emotions, and learn to work through and eliminate those feelings that no longer serve us. By engaging in yoga poses, breath work, and meditation, individual can deepen their spiritual connection and tap into their inner selves. Thus, yoga provides an opportunity for self-reflection and introspection. That connection with the inner self can lead to a greater sense of purpose and meaning in life and an enlightened awareness of the interconnectedness of all beings.

Global health is an area of study, research, and practice that places a priority on improving health and achieving equity in health for all people. Everyone should have the opportunity to live a life that supports good health. Achieving equity in health means addressing social and environmental determinants and eliminating disparities in the health system and health care access. Through generosity, compassion, love, and caring, we create oneness among members of the global family. A lack of medicine, water, and electricity, a shortage of doctors, and prohibitive costs all stand in the way of providing good-quality health care to all. It is reported that half of the world lacks access to essential health services.

There is some good news. The report shows that the 21st century has seen an increase in the number of people able to obtain some key health services, such as immunization and family planning, as well as antiretroviral treatment for HIV and insecticide-treated beds to prevent malaria. Few people are now tipped into extreme poverty than at the turn of the century. Progress, however, is very uneven. There are wide gaps in the availability of service in sub-Saharan Africa and southern Asia. Without optimum health care, how can children reach their full potential? And without a healthy, productive population, how can society realize its aspirations? Every year, nearly 6 million die in developing countries due to the low quality of health care. Strategies for improving health care in developing countries include long-term economic growth, biomedical intervention, improving water sources and sanitation, better diets, improving women's rights and maternal health, providing cheaper drugs, and controlling corporations.

While poor countries suffer from a scarcity of food, rich countries like the U.S. contribute billions of tons of food waste ending up in landfills, emitting greenhouse gases, and exacerbating the global climate crisis. Studies also indicate that if America cut its meat consumption in half, carbon emissions would be slashed significantly. It could also reduce the incidence of obesity, cancer, and other illnesses. Plant-based food is more sustainable and can have a significantly lower carbon footprint by using less overall land, water, and other resources. An increase in the supply of plant-based food will also be available to directly tackle world hunger, help address climate change, and create a more efficient food production to feed the world's growing population.

More prosperous nations tend to have more adequate food supply, better drinking water, better schools, better human rights, and more income equity, as well as a number of other indicators of a higher quality of life. There needs to be a balance between individual and collective well-being. We do not live in isolation. We are a part of the planet Earth.

Bjorn Lomberg, in his book "Best Things First," has outlined 12 efficient solutions for the poor half of the world. Based on peer review research, 12 of the most efficient policies that dramatically improve the lives of people living in the poorest half of the world. For about $35 billion per year, we can save 4.2 million lives annually, and we make the poor half of the world more than a trillion dollars better off each and every year. The author of the study claims that we can almost entirely end tuberculosis, and reduce the death toll of chronic diseases by 1,5 million. Further, we can increase yield in agriculture, make farmers produce more while avoiding hunger for more than a hundred million people. Investment of $35 billion is a tiny fraction of the trillions of dollars we spend on military and weapons of mass destruction throughout the world. In the 20th century, human relations and the sustainability of the planet took a secondary position compared to advances in science and technology. As a result, the disparity between the rich and the poor has been widened.

To address the inequality and further improve health conditions in poor countries, it includes combating hunger, access to clean drinking water, and sanitation. Shawn Paul, in his book Religions, Spirituality and Humanity, describes the humanitarian projects providing material or logistical assistance to a group of people or to a country in need of aid. Humanitarian projects include reducing poverty, providing emergency help in case of natural or man-made disasters, and providing aid to boost the economy. Global Wellness Institute (GWI) empowers wellness worldwide by educating the public and private sectors about preventable health issues and wellness. GWI is a valuable source of guidance and assistance to the poverty-stricken population.

Transcending global well-being, this author fervently envisions a day when all nations, as a global family, will join hands together towards building an egalitarian society where all beings cooperate for the common good of all citizens of the world, where the inherent and intrinsic worth of all humans is recognized. Where all beings have an opportunity to lead a meaningful and purposeful life, I hope this book will inspire readers to lead a harmonious and balanced life.

Glossary

Physical Health

Carbohydrate (Carb)- Food consisting of or containing a lot of sugar, starch, cellulose, or similar substance that can be broken down to release energy in the human body, and makes up one of the main nutrient food groups.

Glycemic index (G.I.)-This refers to how quickly the sugar is released into the bloodstream. Low-G.I. food releases sugar slowly. This gives a prolonged supply of energy to the body.

Fat- Fat is one of the essential nutrients that supply calories to the body. It is a squishy layer that stores energy and protects organs.

Saturated fat- Saturated fat is generally solid at room temperature. It is commonly found in animal products, such as meat, poultry, egg yolk, and dairy products. It is also found in coconut and palm oil. Saturated fat has a negative impact on health. Saturated fat raises blood cholesterol more than anything else in the diet.

Unsaturated fat- Unsaturated fat includes polyunsaturated and monounsaturated fats and omega-3 fats. They will have a positive impact on health.

Monounsaturated fat- Monounsaturated fat is found in greater amounts in foods from plants, including olive oil and canola oil. Monounsaturated fat helps to reduce blood cholesterol.

Polyunsaturated fat- Polyunsaturated fat is a highly unsaturated fat that is found in food products derived from plants, including safflower, sunflower, and soybean oils. Like monounsaturated fat, it is a healthier alternative to saturated fat.

Trans fat- Trans-fats are unsaturated fats that rarely exist in natural food, but are associated with partially hydrogenated oils. They are usually added to process food such as cake and biscuits. Trans fat is harmful to health.

Cholesterol- Cholesterol is an odorless, white, waxy powder. Cholesterol is a compound that is similar to fat. It is needed by the body to form the outside barrier of cells. It can be made both by the liver in the body and consumed through sources in the diet.

Protein- Dietary protein is needed to supply amino acids for the growth and maintenance of our cells and tissues. Lipoproteins are protein-coated packages that carry fat and cholesterol through the body. Lipoproteins are classified by their density.

HDL cholesterol, or high-density lipoprotein, helps carry the "bad cholesterol" away from the walls of the arteries and return it to the bloodstream, thus preventing the buildup of cholesterol in artery walls. That is why it is called good cholesterol.

LDL cholesterol- The "bad cholesterol" or low-density lipoprotein, carries the largest amount of cholesterol in the blood and is responsible for the deposition of cholesterol in the artery walls. An elevated LDL cholesterol level is associated with the risk of heart disease.

Triglycerides- Triglycerides are fat molecules that help in metabolism and moving other fats around the body. High levels of triglycerides, like LDL, can cause plaque buildup in the walls of arteries.

Total cholesterol is the sum of a person's HDL cholesterol, LDL cholesterol, and 20% of their triglyceride.

Atherosclerosis- Atherosclerosis is a type of hardening of the arteries in which cholesterol, particularly LDL, triglycerides, and other blood components, build up in the walls of arteries. As a result, the arteries in the heart may narrow, reducing the flow of oxygen-rich blood and nutrients to the heart.

Coronary heart disease (CHD) is caused by the narrowing of the coronary arteries. It is caused by atherosclerosis. In time, the inadequate supply of oxygen-rich blood leads to chest pain and a heart attack, and can possibly lead to death.

Body mass index (BMI)- Body mass measures weight in relation to height and is universally accepted for the evaluation of body obesity. BMI correlates highly with body fat in most people. Normal healthy BMI is between 18.5 and 24.9.

Glycated Hemoglobin or HbA1C is a blood test that is used to diagnose diabetes. It is also used to monitor blood glucose control in people. Hemoglobin (Hb) is the protein in red blood cells that carries oxygen through your body. The non-diabetic range is below 5/7%. Anyone with an HbA1C value of 5.7to 6.4 is considered pre-diabetic, while a diabetic can be diagnosed with an HbA1C of 6.5% or higher.

Sleep Apnea- Obstructive sleep apnea (OSA) is a disorder in which a person's breathing is obstructed frequently during sleep.

Mental and Emotional Health

Cerebral Cortex- The outer layer of the forebrain. The cerebral cortex is involved in higher-level processes such as thinking, planning, language processing, decision-making, and coordination of motor information. Intellectual functioning, learning new skills, and sharing thoughts come from the cerebral cortex of the brain. Frontal and prefrontal lobes of the cerebral cortex are deeply involved in mental health functions such as cognition, judgment, and logical planning.

Limbic system- The Limbic system is the subcortical functioning in the forebrain and is associated with aspects of emotions, motivation, and memory.

Stress- Stress is a process of adjusting to circumstances that disrupt or threaten to disrupt a person's daily functioning. Stress is an automatic physical reaction to a change or demand.

Eustress- Eustress is a positive stress that inspires one to better meet life challenges.

Distress- The scientific term for excessive or undesirable stress.

Biofeedback- It is a type of mind-body technique used to control some of the body's functions, such as heart rate, breathing pattern, and muscle response.

Mindfulness- Mindfulness is paying attention to one's ongoing experience in a way that allows openness, fully present and aware during activities.

Sternberg's Triangular Theory of Love- This triangular theory of love holds that love can be understood in terms of three components that together can be viewed as forming the vertices of a triangle. These three components are passion, intimacy, and commitment.

Maslow's Hierarchy of innate needs- Maslow's five innate needs in order are physiological, safety and security, love and belongingness, self-esteem, and self-actualization.

Self-efficacy- Self-efficacy is the belief that one can have the ability to perform/or the capacity to learn the behavior necessary for us to reach a desired goal.

Eudaimonia- Eudaimonia is a state of or condition of "good spirit" and which is commonly translated as "happiness". Eudaimonia is a much deeper and richer concept than happiness. The Stoic happiness triangle determines one's wisdom living with virtues, self-control, and personal responsibility blended together, which causes a condition known as Eudaimonia.

Rational Emotive Behavior Therapy (REBT)- REBT is a type of Cognitive Behavior Therapy (CBT) that focuses on changing the irrational thoughts or beliefs that negatively affect a person's emotions or behavior.

Spiritual Health

Self-transcendence- Self-transcendence is the expansion of one's consciousness beyond the self, to something higher.

Purpose and meaning of life- The Purpose of life is to find out who you really are, to grow and evolve, to reach a higher state of consciousness, to experience the Divine, and to become enlightened. Meaning refers to how we make sense of life and roles in it.

References

Baur, Brent. 2024. Mayo Clinic Guide to Holistic Health: Mayo Clinic Press.

Hendricks, Gay. 2000. *Conscious Living:* Harper's Collins: New York.

Kessler, David. 2020. *Fast carbs, Slow Carbs*. Harper Collins: New York.

Krieger, Ellie. 2012. *Small Changes, Big Results*: Clark Potter: New York.

Levey, Joel & Levey, Michelle. 2021. *Living Balance*. Wisdom at Work: Hawaii.

Lomberg, Bjorn. 2023. *Best Things first*. Copenhagen Consensus Centre. Copenhagen.

Mehta, Vipin. 2011. *Global Healing*. Fulbright Publishing. New York.

Mehta, Vipin.2011. *Global Healing. New Vista of Hope.* Fulbright Publishing. New York.

Meyers, D.S. 1992. *The Pursuit of Happiness*. Avon Books. New York.

Paul, Shawn. 2023. *Religions, Spirituality, and Humanity*. Archway Publishing. Indiana.

Paul. Shawn. 2022. *Religion without Boundaries.* Archway Publishing. Indiana.

Pichere, P., & Cadiat, C. 2015.*Maslow's Hierarchy of Needs.* Lemaitre.

Ruff, C.D. 1998. *Psychological well-Being in Adult life- Current Directions.* Psychological Science 4(4), 97-104.

Weiss, Peter. 2023. *More health, less Care*. Create Space. Columbia, S.C.

Wilson, Rainn. 2023. *Soul Boom*. Hachette Book Group. New York.

https://www.heart.org/en/news/2025/01/14/what-is-healthspan-and-how-can-you-maximize-yours www.heart.org

https://www.betterup.com/blog/how-to-improve-social-skills BetterUp

https://www.oxfam.org/richest

https://www.medicalnewstoday.com/articles/282929 Medical News Today

https://www.samhsa.gov

https://www.usnews.com

https://www.betterup.com/blog/how-to-have-good-work-life-balance BetterUp+1

https://www.healthline.com/health/fitness/exercise

Authors Bio

Author Shawn Paul has masters of science degrees in chemistry, fuel science, and clinical psychology. After working for ten years in scientific field, he pursued and completed his master degree in clinical psychology. He has worked as a psychotherapist over 30 years, including 25 years in private practice. His practice focused on individual and group therapy. Helping others to overcome life struggles and difficulties has been a rewarding experience for Shawn Paul. Since his retirement, he has become interested in reading, writing, travelling and service to humanity. He has published two books Religion without Boundaries and Religions, spirituality, and Humanity. This is his third book on Harmony and Balance in Living. Shawn Paul has travelled with his wife covering five continents and over thirty countries. He passionately believes in helping others and gives financial assistance to many charitable institutions.

Shawn Paul is happily married, and has two grown up children and one grandchild. He balances his life integrating his professional life with family life.

www.ingramcontent.com/pod-product-compliance
Lightning Source LLC
Chambersburg PA
CBHW041116120626
46547CB00019B/2738